Writing Across the Curriculum Pamphlets

Project Team 1971-76

Nancy Martin, *Director*

Peter Medway

Harold Smith

Pat D'Arcy

Bryan Newton

Robert Parker

James Britton,
 *ongoing adviser and Chairman
 of the Consultative Committee*

Writing Across the Curriculum Pamphlets

edited by Nancy Martin

A Selection from the Schools Council
and London University Institute of Education
Joint Project: Writing Across the Curriculum

BOYNTON/COOK PUBLISHERS, INC.
UPPER MONTCLAIR, NEW JERSEY 07043

These pamphlets were first published individually in 1973, 1974, and 1975 by the Project: Writing Across the Curriculum: Schools Council/London University Institute of Education English Department and subsequently by Ward Lock Educational. © Schools Council Publications. All are reprinted by permission of the Schools Council. All rights reserved. No part of this book may be used or reproduced in any manner without written permission except in the case of brief quotations embodied in critical articles and reviews.

Acknowledgements
To the students and staff of the following schools—our thanks for all their help: Chelsea School, London; Crown Woods School, London; Walworth School, London; Countesthorpe College, Leicestershire; Mount Grace High School, Hinckley; St. Paul's Secondary School, Bessbrook, Northern Ireland. Thanks are due also to Walter Drews, Principal of Wansfell College, Essex, for his generous cooperation, and to all the participants in the Science and Humanities Seminars held at Wansfell College in 1974 and 1975.

For information address Boynton/Cook Publishers, Inc., P.O. Box 860, 52 Upper Montclair Plaza, Upper Montclair, NJ. 07043.

ISBN 0-86709-101-0 (original pamphlets ISBN numbers: 0-7062-3564-9, 3566-5, 3565-7, 3567-3, 3568-1, 3569-X)

Printed in the United States of America

84 85 86 87 88   10 9 8 7 6 5 4 3 2 1

Contents

Introduction Nancy Martin   1

From Information to Understanding: What Children Do with New Ideas
Nancy Martin, Peter Medway, Harold Smith   4

Why Write?
Nancy Martin, Peter Medway, Harold Smith, Pat D'Arcy   34

From Talking to Writing
Peter Medway   60

Keeping Options Open: Writing in the Humanities
Pat D'Arcy   86

from **Writing in Science**
"Science: Writing and Understanding—Writing and Learning"
Sue Watts   114
"Worksheets—My Changing Attitudes Towards Them"
Jeff Shapland   120

from **Language and Learning in the Humanities**
"A Language for Life—or School?"
Bryan Newton   125
"Cooperative Learning"
Peter Medway and Ivor Goodson   132

Introduction

Nancy Martin

Three Teachers, a Program, and a Theory

The project began in September 1971 with a team of three teachers and a theory of writing based on an earlier research program—*The Development of Writing Abilities 11 to 18 years.* Our brief was to take the findings of this earlier research about the relation of writing to learning into schools and work out with teachers how writing might contribute to learning in the various subjects.

We had four kinds of contacts with teachers:

Schools we worked in—necessarily rather few;
Schools we visited—rather more;
Schools we corresponded with—many;
Areas where we held discussion meetings—many.

The Fourth Element.

It was clear to us that three teachers, the program, and the theory had to have a fourth element—print. But what kind of print? Something to go in the pocket, we thought; eight inches by six perhaps, and 24 to 28 pages with large print and headings. Something to take to meetings and to send to corresponding schools; something to read through and argue about and use. It was ideas we were involved with, and ideas restructure other ideas and can't be wholly carried in the head. In short, we needed something that would be part of an ongoing dialogue between the project team and the teacher we were working with. We thought we needed to do a bit at a time—to take the questions that were dominant with the teachers and write about them in relation to our theory in separate pamphlets.

Our First Pamphlet: a Prototype

Our first pamphlet was about information. It was called *From Information to Understanding: What Children Do with New*

Ideas. Most of the teachers we met were much concerned with their students learning things; almost every lesson had its quota of information, and teachers made great efforts to get it learned *and understood.* So our first pamphlet consisted of examples of children using talk and writing to understand the new ideas they met in lessons. Our commentary identified their errors of understanding as they became apparent in what they said, and pointed up how their thinking was restructured as they talked.

We also put forward in this pamphlet the matter of expressive writing. We had found much school writing to be either records of work done or formal little pieces of impersonal writing. Yet, if writing was to work in the way we had shown talk working as an exploratory medium for new ideas, it had to be much looser, and to engage the children's imagination about the possibilities of what they were learning for people or events or processes.

So this pamphlet contained a long stretch of dialogue between two boys (with rare interjections from a teacher), an extended monologue, and two pieces of imaginative writing based on a history lesson. We think these examples, together with our commentary, demonstrated the way learning was going on with the all-powerful aid of language. It is not easy to catch learning on the wing, but we think the examples in this pamphlet do this.

Subsequent Pamphlets: Punch Lines of Theoretical Ideas Exemplified in Mini-profiles

Subsequent pamphlets took up the issues of genuine communications, not dummy runs; of the importance of a sense of audience to writing; of the different kinds of writing according to purposes; of the relation of talking to writing; and of keeping the writers' own options open (individual concerns and intentions) as students move towards the information-crammed examination years.

Thus, the pamphlets developed out of work in progress and the recurrent theme was how writing was, in some cases, helping children learn, or in others, limiting or even preventing learning.

The Second Stage.

Later in the project it became clear to us that we had to move into a new phase in which teachers themselves did the writing. We had tackled the general issues of the relation of language to learning, but the applications in the various subjects had to be done by the teachers of those subjects. We therefore arranged two weekend seminars, one for ten to twelve science teachers, and one of the same size for teachers of humanities (social science and English). A day was spent discussing and a day drafting in groups of two or three. The outcomes were the two pamphlets (50 to 60 pages), *Writing in Science* and *Language and Learning in the Humanities.* We have included two articles from each of these in the present collection.

A Long, Slow Process.

The notion that writing can be an instrument of learning, of reflection, of discovery, rather than merely a means of recording or testing is well understood by writers, but hardly understood at all by teachers, students, or parents. For this new orientation to take hold on people's thinking (and practice) is a long, slow task, but the recognition that in developing writing we are into the development of learning is gaining ground, particularly in the United States as a result of the National Writing Projects. The focus on teachers' writing, and thereby learning about learning through their own writing, has made remarkable changes in their attitudes and procedures. The British Writing Across the Curriculum pamphlets were produced in similar circumstances but have the advantage of being rooted in a learning theory developed from a related research project. They have a high relevance for the current situation in the United States.

From Information to Understanding:
What Children Do with New Ideas

Nancy Martin, Peter Medway, and Harold Smith

Writing is employed as an educational activity in most areas of the curriculum. The writing of notes, essays, stories, summaries, poems, answers, personal narratives and so on is a major component of education, in terms both of the time, energy and materials devoted to it and of the importance ascribed to it by teachers.

It is important that such a central educational process should be made as effective as it can be: this means, certainly, that children's writing abilities need to be developed to the full but also, and perhaps for most teachers of more immediate importance, that writing should be used in such a way as to make its maximum possible contribution to *learning*.

In the endeavour to achieve this, we would want to use relevant research. But much research into language is necessarily descriptive, and therefore there is a secondary job to be done of drawing out its implications for practice. The present Project has such a job to do. We are concerned with a particular piece of research, a five year investigation into the development of writing abilities over the years 11 to 18 which was conducted under the auspices of the Schools Council by the Writing Research Unit of the University of London Institute of Education. We want to 'operationalise' the findings of this research: that is, to work out how they bear on what teachers actually do with writing, to construct a theoretical justification for existing good practice and to consider possible new ways of working; in other words to contribute to the building of a rationale for school procedure with regard to writing.

Such an undertaking can only be conducted jointly by researchers and teachers of different subjects, since the theoretical understandings about the writing process have to be related to the purposes and procedures of teachers in all areas of the curriculum. Our procedure is therefore to work with teachers in a number of schools and together to take the findings of the research and in the light of them interpret the writing activities which are occurring in the schools and analyse what they are achieving, and to devise and try out alternative possibilities; and then to make our conclusions more widely available through publications, conferences, meetings etc.

It is however our hope that this enquiry will by no means be confined to those teachers with whom the Project team is directly involved, but that an ongoing and widening discussion will take place in schools, local centres and subject associations.

We see our publications, of which this is the first, as a contribution to such discussion. They are likely to take a variety of forms: some will be more polished than others; some will be as long as this, some much shorter; some (we hope) will be written by teachers. They will include reports of work in schools, discussion of writing procedures in particular school subjects and comment on wider curriculum issues.

This paper is our first attempt to relate the theoretical ideas of the Writing Research to the objectives of different areas of the curriculum, and is offered for discussion. It arises, in fact, from discussion we have had with teachers with whom we have been working in three schools. It does not attempt any systematic exposition of the Writing Research, though its central ideas derive from it, but instead looks at a very general concern, one shared by teachers of most subjects, the contribution language can make in moving from new information to deeper understanding.

We said 'language' rather than 'writing' because writing specifically will not be at the centre of attention this time: rather we want to place writing in the context of the use of language in general. We examine the process that occurs when children use language to learn with: this process is more accessible to the observer when it takes place in *talk*, so our main examples will be of children talking. This will enable us to distinguish between the features of verbal discourse in general which are relevant to learning and the particular contribution which may be made by writing.

Our topic is, then, what is involved in the learning of new ideas and what is the part language can play in the process. Our procedure is to ask the questions about some actual cases. We take a number of children, working in different school subjects, at a point where information has been presented to them and they are taking it on from there.

We start with two boys, Robert and Terry, aged 12. They are having a discussion with an interviewer. With the aid of books and worksheets they have been studying the Upper Thames area and its early inhabitants. Of the facts they have been presented with, the following are important for what follows:

> The rock of the hills where the Thames begins is limestone. Limestone is a porous rock: that is, water soaks down into it. Therefore there is little moisture on the surface and little grows on it.
> The valleys on the other hand used to be thickly forested. Early man could till the light soil on the hills and grow wheat and barley, but could not cope with the thick forests in the valleys.

These ideas would not at first sight appear to present much difficulty, except perhaps for the idea of 'porous' — and that is explained. One might think this is the sort of information which could be taken straight over and added effortlessly to one's stock of knowledge — to learn it, it would almost be enough simply to be told it. What Robert wrote in answer to some worksheet questions would tend to confirm this view:

The Thames is a river that goes through london in to other parts of england. It starts in cotswolds, the highlands. the thames starts in rock, the rock is limestone. In london the thames meanders its way through.

The cotswold stone is limestone. Limestone was formed millions of years ago and was found at the bottom of the sea. Chalk is a very soft limestone so is marble*, limestone is a porous rock and it soaks up water. it was formed with other rocks mixing up.

The thames valley was covered in thick forest and so were other places. But in high hills there was chalk and limestone and the water was drained into low ground so there were hardly any trees.

This is a fairly accurate account; his use of the notion of porosity makes sense. So we can say that, at one level at least, the information has 'got home'. According to one common way of thinking, the learning could now be said to have been achieved.

That might easily have been all that happened to the information, but in this case the interviewer invited Robert to recall it. He asked Robert what he now knew as a result of doing the work, and Robert told him, producing very much the same sort of statement as he had made in his writing, and leading us again to suppose, 'Yes, he's got it'. Then there was a silence, confirming the sense that everything had been said. The interviewer then gave Terry a lead, and a conversation started between the boys. Everything, it seems, had not been said.

Here is the first part of the transcript:

1	Interviewer	Robert, what have you learnt by doing this latest worksheet? What do you know now that you didn't know before?
2	Robert	About er, the Iron Age, and the Stone Age, and things like that. About the weapons they had and things, and about the er they had to go to er you know places where there weren't any forests, which was quite hard, so they had to go

* Presumeably he means that marble is a limestone (which it is), not that it's very soft.

		in the high hills where there was porous rock, and the water soaked through to the bottom so no trees could grow.
3	Terry	What shall I say?
4	Interviewer	Well, have you got any comments on what he's said?
5	Terry	Er, about the porous rock. If there was a porous rock, then lots of birds and that would sit on it to drink and that, and probably do their droppings at the . . . so that trees and plants and that would grow there. Instead of soaking right through, you get some plants up there.
6	Robert	You wouldn't get any plants up there because the porous rock would soak it through. It wouldn't stay at the top. So birds *wouldn't* be about, any moisture at all.
7	Terry	Yes, well some of the water might stay on top.
8	Robert	No, not in porous rock.
9	Terry	Well, how do you think the birds lived?
10	Robert	Don't know really, I suppose they'd go to a different part of the country, wouldn't they. Different country . . .
11	Terry	They must have lived on something. And drank.
12	Robert	Well, they would have gone down near the bottom of the hill, you know, or somewhere where the water comes out, where the water comes out . . . when it goes down to the bottom it soaks into the bottom so you'll find more forests at the bottom of the hill than the top of the hill, 'cause there's more porous rock at the top. In the, er, there was, then, it's told in the book . .
13	Terry	Up to now there's lots of caves where the stone age used to live and mainly, millions of years ago, these were made by water, soaking through the rocks, porous rocks and that and it made these caves, in the stone.
14	Robert	So water would soak through to the er to the you know hole, makes a hole in the, you know, soak through there

15	Terry	and it would come out somewhere and make a stream
16	Robert	and it would push, push, the water would push a great big gigantic hole in the rock and then stream down to you know to the bottom of the hill.
17	Interviewer	Have you seen any caves like that?
18	Robert Terry	No

So the knowledge, which Robert at first sets out for the interviewer as if saying, 'There it is — so what?' gets activated: it is put to use and tested, and in the process is extended and reshaped.

To track the main developments: Terry (5) because he has some idea of porous rock being able to hold water so that birds can drink it, challenges Robert's statement (2). The challenge forces Robert to *use* the knowledge he has: Robert's sources told him nothing about the presence or absence of birds, but he can deduce from what he knows that there wouldn't be any (6). (He is of course wrong, because the general idea that he is working from — that *all* the water sinks down, leaving none at the surface — is an over simple one. We discuss the question of error later.) In answering Terry's further point (9), he suggests (12) the birds would go to the bottom of the hills for water, thus applying his knowledge again. But this time his information proves inadequate: he discovers as he talks that he does not know why or how there is water at the bottom of the hill. First he says confidently that the water 'comes out' at the bottom of the hill, then says it again as if having a second look at the idea and sensing problems. When he had said earlier (2) that 'water sinks through the rock', he had added, automatically, 'to the bottom'. Sinking through to the bottom and coming out is the sort of picture that derives from watering plants and the water coming out of the hole at the bottom of the plant pot. But what would 'the bottom of the rock' mean? We talk about 'the bottom of the hill', meaning the valley, but that's the bottom of the visible outside slope, not the underneath surface of the rock — if there is one. Robert doesn't solve this here but becomes aware of it as a problem. To cope with this gap in his knowledge, he explains ''cause there's more porous rock at the top', which isn't a satisfying solution but is the best he can do for the moment.

As they learnt it, their information did not refer to caves, but they both already know something about them and want to bring the new information about water in porous rock into line with their vague existing knowledge about caves being formed by water. Terry raises the issue and Robert senses an incompatibility between his information about water *soaking* down through the rock and the sort of *vigorous* action necessary to make a cave. To resolve the problem he proposes a hypothesis (16) involving some sort of build-up of pressure bursting a hole in the side of the hill.

So the *implications* of the information are being drawn, and old knowledge is being brought out and looked at afresh in the light of the new. Inconsistencies and gaps are being revealed in the course of talking, and are either resolved by new hypotheses or left unsolved: in either case, and whether the hypotheses are right or wrong, progress has been made because the mind is now as it were pre-set to be receptive to relevant new information when it comes along — whether it be the sight of grass and birds on Salisbury Plain, or of a stream pouring from a hillside, or verbal information to the same effect.

That some of their ideas — both ones they bring with them and ones they produce now — are wrong, we have already seen.

In the section that follows we can plot the process by which each boy's errors become apparent (to himself and to the other) and are then corrected. In other words, we shall now observe a central educational process at work. (Two main issues are dealt with in this section: whether anything can grow on porous rock, and what is meant by the softness of porous rock. It's a lengthy stretch of transcript, but it seemed better to give it in one go than to break it up.)

19	Interviewer	What would you say 'porous' means then?
20	Terry	It means that it's not a hard base, it's a very soft one and it's like a sponge, and when you drop water on it it soaks in. It's like sand and dirt and that, when you drop a piece of water on it it soaks around.

21	Robert	And then there's a harder forms of sand, that, if you found any quicksand, if you dropped anything there you'd start falling in, soaking in, 'cause that's what the water did, water's soaked into the er sand and made it much softer. And it you know made a kind of forever hole in it, the sand filled it up, and made it all muddy water, so if anybody stepped on it, or anything went on it

(A discussion of quicksand follows, which we omit.)

22	Interviewer	Anyway, going back to the porous rock, are you both saying then that nothing will grow on porous rock?
23	Robert	No, most things need water
24	Terry	No, I'm saying that it *will* grow on porous rock because if it's a wet rock then things will grow on it because they need moisture, and water, to live.
25	Robert	It's like saying that something can grow on a sponge then
26	Terry	Yes. Well, there's earth on the porous rock, isn't there. There must be a lot of earth and er
27	Robert	Yes, but earth needs moisture. And moisture . . . (inaudible)
28	Terry	like er shamrock, that grows in er on rock and that, don't it.
29	Robert	Yes, you find
30	Interviewer	What does?
31	Terry	Shamrocks. Some plants grow on rock, don't they?
32	Robert	If you dug far enough on porous rock, you know, on porous rock, you know, if you dug far enough, you'd be able to grow things, but otherwise you haven't got enough moisture at the top.

(Section omitted — they say they haven't seen the cliffs of Dover.)

33	Interviewer	You've seen other chalk cliffs?
34	Terry	Yes

35	Interviewer	Now on the top of the cliffs, was anything growing?
36	Terry	Yes, grass and er some trees, very rarely, but I did see some grass and that growing on it
37	Interviewer	Yes, in fact grass does grow on top of chalk and limestone. Er — but not, you wouldn't get forests growing. There's some, there's some water is held at the top. You see, if it rains it takes a bit of time for the water to soak down, right down into the chalk, so while it's going down, that's sometimes time enough for plants to get all the moisture they need out of it. So there's enough for grass to grow. And then the surface
38	Robert	There isn't enough for trees.
39	Interviewer	Right.
		(further explanation by interviewer omitted)
40	Interviewer	Now you said right at the beginning, Robert, that these early men chose to live up on the top of the porous rock, and not down in the valleys.
41	Terry	But if they did, the rain would soak them down, they'd sink gradually and sink and sink, if it was a porous rock, 'cause it'd be
42	Interviewer	What would sink?
43	Terry	The house, if they . . . if they was living there.
44	Robert	Houses. They didn't make proper houses did they?
45	Terry	No, tents.
46	Interviewer	No, it's not like sponge. I mean, it's wrong to think of it as like sponge. Porous rock's more like, I mean it's like a piece of chalk. You dip it in the ink
47	Terry	It'll go blue
48	Interviewer	Yes, it'll go blue all the way through. But it doesn't collapse, does it. It's still hard, even when it's full of water, well, chalk rock is like that. It stays hard all right. But it's just that it's got a lot of holes in it, little holes

49	Robert	Yes, I know, it's like a piece of carbon, punch a lot of hole in it
50	Interviewer	Yes, or expanded polystyrene, it's like that
51	Robert	And it hasn't got big holes, it's got holes that you can't even see, unless you look too closely, with a microscope or something you'd be able to see some of the bigger holes. But er
52	Interviewer	You would, yes.
53	Robert	but they chose to live up there because they could go down the valley when they wanted to grow things in the fields. In the fields they only had to go to the top, in fact, because grass would grow, and they'd be able to grow the smaller things.
54	Interviewer	Like
55	Robert	Like wheat and barley and oats and you know little things anyway and corn, and er so they didn't need to go down, if they went down in the valley they wouldn't have any warmth or anything, 'cause too many things would be growing quite quickly, 'cause the, you know, they'd be growing because of water down there
56	Terry	Yes, but down at the bottom the water's sunk through porous rock and it makes underground streams along the bottom.
57	Robert	I know
58	Terry	How do you think that they get their water?
59	Robert	They get it from, because, doesn't all make water, it, if it makes underground streams, let's say that's, that's the top, well some of it would soak just a bit over, wouldn't it, would soak into the soil anyway
60	Terry	There'd be some streams, but not on the top.
61	Robert	Whether there's streams or not, they'd soak the soil, wouldn't they, with er water. So it would go, rise, wouldn't it, the water would make the whole lot of the soil like a sponge, er, not like a sponge really, yes, like a sponge, because er you know you dip anything, you know a sponge,

		just a little bit, it'll go up the top wouldn't it, go all the way through
62	Terry	Yes but what do you think they make their houses out of?

The point about having abstract and general knowledge, and the reason so much importance is attached to it in school, is that from it we can derive or deduce information about particular cases that we've never explicitly been told about. We can take it with us into new situations and it enables us to understand them and make predictions about them. The power of such knowledge is manifested in the capacity to *generate* information in new and unpredicted situations: conversely, it is often in applying abstract knowledge to particular realities in order to explain and predict that inadequacies in it are revealed. Here we have a good example of this: the weakness of Terry's knowledge of porous rock becomes clear not when he states it at the abstract level ('it's not a hard base' etc. (20)) but when he uses it to *derive* the prediction that houses would sink in porous rock. This idea is easily seen to be wrong and the interviewer then becomes aware of the underlying misunderstanding and corrects it.

So this example shows how inadequacies in general concepts may be shown up when the concepts are put to use in the course of talking. It also shows very well a particular way in which a concept may be inadequate, and the sort of adjustment that is required to correct it. It's clear from what Terry says that he not only thinks that porous rock is soft (which it is — compared with granite) and like a sponge (which it is — in that it absorbs water) but that it is actually *soft like a sponge*, or like mud. His hang-up is that he's always understood rock to be 'hard': so on being told that this particular sort of rock is soft he takes it to be different from the rock he is familiar with. Putting this misconception right is a matter of revising his concept of soft/hard, perhaps changing it from a simple opposition to a scale with hard rock at one end, mud and sponges at the other and chalk somewhere in the middle, soft as rock goes but still harder than mud.

To correct the misunderstanding which has now become apparent the interviewer feeds in new information (37, 40 and 48). What happens to it? Look at what Robert does.

From Information to Understanding

In the first place he immediately wants to *complete* it for himself: he takes the statement that 'it's got a lot of holes in it' (48) and *visualises* for himself what it must be like. When he says (51)

> And it hasn't got big holes, it's got holes that you can't even see, unless you look too closely, with a microscope or something you'd be able to see some of the bigger holes.

we have to take it that he is not saying something he definitely knows — nobody's ever actually told him that chalk has microscopic holes — but is *surmising* — 'This is how it must be'; it seems he's using what he knows about some *other* substance as a basis for informed speculation or hypothesising about chalk.

Secondly, he discovers implications in the new information which affect what he had thought before. And he discovers them *only as he talks* almost as if tripping up over them. The interviewer has explained (37) that *although* water tends to pass through rock leaving the top dry, nevertheless the *soil* holds enough water for grass — but not trees — to grow. Robert (53) makes a statement which hasn't taken this into account:

> but they chose to live up there because they could go down the valley when they wanted to grow things in the fields.

He is still thinking that nothing grows on the hills so that the fields must be in the valley. But now, remembering what the interviewer has said, he reformulates.('In fact' signals a correction.)

> In the fields they only had to go to the top, in fact, because grass would grow, and they'd be able to grow the smaller things
> Like?
> Like wheat and barley and oats and you know little things anyway and corn, and er so they didn't need to go down.

So that it is only in the act of articulating what he thinks that he realises what is implied in the new information.

This leads him to make a compensating adjustment to his concept of the valley (55) — it's not a useful but a hostile environment because the rich vegetation (caused by the plentiful water) would make it cold (a hypothesis).

Terry sees a problem in this (56): the water would be in *underground* streams: how then would it be available for plants? In response Robert produces a new hypothesis which somehow explains the presence of water by permeation through the *soil*, and doesn't depend on streams, but is cut off by Terry (62) who suddenly changes the subject to one of his own concerns.

There are many more points we could make about this discussion, but the essential one is that getting hold of information is not such a simple operation as is implied by that expression (or its equivalents — 'aquiring' concepts, 'grasping' ideas, etc). Information is not just taken on like cargo. Nor is it like being given something, as if now you have something where before you had nothing. Information isn't stuff. We can see from the transcript that when information is received it doesn't drop into an empty pigeonhole but comes up against what is there already — namely, other knowledge, more or less clear and explicit — and a process has to occur of marrying the new with the old. The new may be interpreted in the light of the old or the old may be modified to take account of the new.

We can't really be said to know something until we've made it part of our way of thinking and explored its implications for related areas of knowledge. Often this involves shaking-up and reorganising a whole system of ideas by which we explain the world to ourselves — and this 're-forming of the theory' goes far beyond any notion suggested by terms like 'getting' and 'acquiring'. 'Passive learning' is a happily discredited idea: but it's important to realise that the 'active' in 'active learning' refers less to finding information for yourself than to what you do with it when you've found it.

The transcript shows us how many things have to be brought into play in coming to understand what at first appears a relatively uncomplicated set of ideas. It also shows what a lengthy and time-consuming business it is — all these words and all that time to deal with what is after all a very tiny part of school knowledge. And yet it seems to be indispensible: without the talk the boys would have been carrying round misconceptions and ignorances of which they were unaware, and the information they had 'learnt', not having been worked over and assimilated, would probably have been forgotten. Yet how many children in relation to how much of their curriculum have the opportunity *really* to learn in this sort of way?

It might be objected that in any sixth form we could find students who had a real understanding and knowledge and yet had hardly ever 'chewed over' ideas in this way with other people in the course of their work. The answer would seem to be not that the chewing-over process has not occurred but that it has occurred internally: in other words, the students have been thinking. But if we consider that very large number of pupils for whom most of school knowledge never really becomes part of their view of the world but instead withers and dies, the reason may indeed be that the process has not occurred – not in any form. We might have more success with such children if we deliberately made provision for this thinking, chewing-over part of learning to go on openly: which is to say, in language.

We can see by looking at what the two boys did what it was they needed to do, and in retrospect realise how far short Robert's brief *written* answers came of fulfilling those needs. Going back to them, we notice above all the brevity and *closed* quality of those answers. They sound confident in their knowledge; their sentences are well formed; they have an air of finality. (Terry's, which we didn't quote, were even shorter, equally confident in tone and mainly wrong.) But what they both *needed* to do, as we have seen, was to speculate, hypothesise, relate, explore – not to assert as if they were telling us something new what they had just got from the book.

The qualities of their *talk* on the other hand seem ideally fitted to the job of relating to new information. In the first place it seems a much more suitable medium than those short written pronouncements. This sort of expressive, informal talk, conducted by people who know each other, can carry the movement of thought as it occurs – the galvanisings, the scanning for clues, the rapid switches of focus, the dawnings of awareness. Loosely structured, uneven in pace, full of stumblings, false starts and half finished sentences — and the more markedly so the newer the ground being broken — it's the natural vehicle for the first draft of our ideas. (It is only when we are confident in what we are saying that our discourse tends to be well-constructed, even and urbane.)

> and it would push, push, the water would push a great big gigantic hole in the rock and then stream down to you know to the bottom of the hill (16).
>
> If you dug far enough on porous rock, you know, on porous rock, you know, if you dug far enough, you'd be able to grow things, but otherwise you haven't got enough moisture at the top (32).

Secondly, the talking situation seems to produce a motivation that is absent from the written answers. Perhaps it is not surprising that Terry felt no great commitment to making accurate formulations in response to mere printed questions. How different it is with the formulations they make *for each other*. Every statement is made as it were from an exposed position and is liable to be challenged: there is a premium attached to getting it right. We need to inform ourselves of the sorts of situations in which children do care about getting it right, about checking the report against the reality to confirm that it is as they've said it is.

Can we make talk like this a regular classroom activity? In this case an adult was present with the two boys; but such an arrangement isn't always necessary. (On the other hand let's not be too hasty in dismissing it as impractical: are we really using all the adults available? Students? Other adults — do they have to be experts?) Provided they were prepared to be serious about it — and many children are — these boys could probably have got a long way without the interviewer. If we isolate what the adult has contributed we find it is mainly new information or corrections to misunderstandings: on the whole he responds rather than initiates, and most of their formulations are made at *each other's* prompting. Most of the *questions* come from them. So potentially they might have covered a fair part of the ground on their own.

Here is an example of two other boys (also aged 12) who were on their own and who were serious about it. We quote it partly to illustrate what can happen without an adult, partly to advance our enquiry by showing information being operated on in another way. The boys asked for a tape-recorder, took it into a room on their own and read various things from their folders into it. As part of their work on India they had each written a story about the Aryans, who struggled over the Himalayas and down into the warm Indus valley, where they destroyed the city of Mohenjo-Daro. They have just finished reading these stories.

Robin   That's a good one.

John   Oh, you've described more of the mountains, I've just des . . . I've just done the battle.

Robin   Yes, so really we've just done about the same, because I've described the mountains and you've described the battles.

John   Yes, so in fact we both, it worked out better, didn't it.

Robin   Yes.

John   Well what do you think type of climate it is in India?

Robin   Must be all snowy on the Himalayas and when they got down there, you know, it's sunny.

John   Well, it depends, don't it, if they're right next to the Himalayas it might not be so sunny, it might be still a bit cold and yet, 'cause of the snow off the Himalayas.

Robin   Yes.

John   And you know, as they go, as the monsoon winds go to the Himalayas they might make the snow and it'll snow just before they get to the Himalayas.

Robin   Yes, and where I put the snowstorm that would be right, wouldn't it.

John   Yes.

Robin   It's blow all the snow up.

John   Yes. And not only that, it might even bring the water in from the . . . well, it depends what time of year it is, don't it, really.

Robin   Yes.

John   But they would have, really, because you know, the wind blows in, brings clouds in with it and then instead of falling as rain they can't 'cause it's so cold it changes into snow.

Robin   Yes. And er they probably lost a lot of men.

John   No, I don't think they did.

Robin   Going round them little pathways.

John   Oh yeah, they might have lost it there but I don't think they did in the battle because

Robin   No

John   the people that they attacked were peace-loving people. They didn't know anything about war, did they. They just liked settling down and being happy and everything.

Robin   Yes.

What concerned them was that the facts in their stories should be correct. 'Where I put the snowstorm, that would be right, wouldn't it?' This leads them to check what they've said about a particular imagined situation against the (general) knowledge derived from the teaching they've received. So the context in which this knowledge gets used — and thereby more deeply learnt — is a literary creation — very different from the situation of Robert and Terry; but the type of talk — loosely-structured, speculative, hypothesising — is the same.

We've now looked at two examples of quite impressive intellectual enquiry which proceeded in talk. We've said quite a bit about one element in these discussions: the type of language the speakers use. We've called it expressive. We've noted also that a certain commitment to 'getting it right' seems to result from another element, the fact that the speakers are in dialogue. Let us say some more about this.

As a vehicle for the sort of learning we've been discussing, dialogue has obvious strengths. Each participant continually forces the other to articulate what he thinks, to cope with awkward facts or arguments, to illustrate and exemplify, to operate on ground not of his own choosing: there is never any problem of what to say next, because if one is silent the other will speak; there is instant feedback which tells you whether you have made yourself clear and presents you with other relevant considerations which you have not so far taken into account.

On the other hand there are limitations: you may often not have the space you would like to expand your ideas, you are in constant danger of being cut off, and the other's interests may divert the conversation away from the area you were beginning to get to grips with.

So if 're-forming your theory' is what we see learning as, then we would expect that it might typically be in dialogue that the sudden insights are achieved which give a notion of how the modified theory will have to go; and parts of the new theory may be provisionally sketched out there and then. But it may also be necessary to set out the theory *in extenso*, rather than piecemeal as the shifting agenda of a conversation demands it. In such a task the active involvement of another person could be a hindrance: one needs a space to work in in which one is not going to be interrupted. So monologue would seem the appropriate mode of discourse: and written monologue would be superior in two respects to spoken, in that there is no pressure of time and in that it is possible to look back at what one has already said and thus control the overall shape of the structure.

But: no gains without corresponding cost. Monologue is more difficult to sustain than dialogue: this is because, due to the very feature that gives it its power — the lack of a participating interlocutor — the speaker gets no feedback (not at any rate in verbal form, and in written monologue not at all). When we write we speak into an empty room in the dark with no one to help us — small wonder children often fall silent after two or three lines.

We proceed then to look at a monologue and we will be concerned with two things: for the re-forming of the theory that we've suggested needs to go on under the impact of new information, what scope does monologue offer? And how, given the difficulties, is monologue sustained? The piece we examine needs once again to be a successful one — we're interested in the *possibilities* of the medium, not its typical accomplishments — and because we want the process of composing to be as evident as it can be we choose a *spoken* monologue, but one that is like writing in one respect, that nobody else was there when it was spoken — only a tape recorder.

The speaker is an 11 year old boy, Trevor; he is in a cloakroom on his own with a tape recorder composing a talk that he is going to give to a group from his class on the subject of the development of man. With the rest of the class he has attended a 'lead lecture' on the subject by one of the teachers, but he has also (unlike his colleagues) spent a lot of time with library books learning more.

> The ice age . . . the temperature . . . as a matter of fact all the dinosaurs were dead, the temperature of our earth began to warm all the ice, glaciers and everything that had come down from the north pole sort of slowly went back sort of thing and melted up. Now the mammals, we had mammals as you know, that had survived, had the use of four legs at this moment. But they sort of learnt, it's funny how, I couldn't explain — they sort of walked a bit you know on their hind legs, you know, only occasionally. It was a sort of creature very much like a, oh let me think, a sort of . . . sort of thing, you know, bent down on four things, on four legs, like — but it sort of went up on two legs when it could. Now this mammal, it wasn't . . . vigorous. It was sort of above the others if you know what I mean. It was cleverer. It could do things better than the others.
>
> Now you see this sort of apish thing began to develop in more than one way. It was developing to walk on its hind legs very stooped, so that it went down on its four legs occasionally, but it also, what else was developing, which was apart from the dinosaurs that was developed and some of the other mammals, it developed in its brain. Its brain developed very, it sort of developed with its body, you know, it went with its body. It hadn't developed without its, it hadn't left its body or its body hadn't left its brain — like a dinosaur, you

know, it was too big and like a (?) or something. It was too big. It had such a small brain, because the brain hadn't grown with the body sort of thing, if you know what I mean.

Now the good thing about the dino — the apish, sort of gorilla thing was that its brain was also developing in a small way and it was learning how to make use of the things around it, not just like the dinosaur made use of plants and ate them. It learnt how to make a home and live in something. Now say it came to a hole in the ground it would know that there he could find shelter. Now if you saw a dinosaur saw a great big cave, a cave in front of it and it knew it could live in it, it wouldn't because it's just stupid. It wouldn't even know that it could live in it. And, see, these gorilla-like things knew that they could live in somewhere sheltered and it would save them about the wind and all the things around them. Now that was a very clever thing.

Now these were advancing slowly and through millions and millions of years we sort of end up with — it still stooped a lot, a very big face sort of thing, very much like a monkey let's say, or a gorilla again. Now these apes or gorillas or monkeys — I don't care what you want to call them — I'll call them apes, I think — apes, learnt all about the world and that they could make use if they thought. They used their brain because they had a brain and they had it, and it was big enough for their body. They thought to themselves we must use the world. They thought it, like, like this. Let's put it like this. Well, we might as well not be sitting on our backsides letting the world spin round and — well, they didn't know about that side — letting the world be here with all the trees and things, we must be able to make something out of it.

Now at this time this sort of things had begun to lose some of their hair that they had and they used, lived in caves. Now they ate a lot of vegetables at the time but now very cleverly they thought all these animals, things around them, could be used to eat. And they used, they caught a rabbit in a sort of, put a, made a sort of hole with their hands and any little rabbit that they could catch and pounce on in time they would use it. They eat it raw, just skin it off and eat it raw, and some of the things that — this is what made them very clever the apes — was that it hadn't much hair left any more, just sort of thin bunchy thing, and it used the skin of what it pulled off to keep itself warm. Now, this was the first inclothed man in an animal and animals and how they began to learn how to move around and live.

Now these animals, these animals, they were still a sort of animal, began to learn how to make huts and things, and they developed in a very funny way. They sort of learnt to live with what was round them. Now the greatest development that they ever made was fire which I will tell you how they discovered later on. It would seem they, these had learnt how to live with the world and they had the intelligence that they used it. Now they was the rulers of the earth from that time on.

Now these animals couldn't make out how to keep themselves alive, and when they — say that they was attacked. They couldn't really figure out what they was meant to do except run. And eventually they thought, why not try and fight back again, and they learnt how to, if a wild boar or pig attacked them, they could get a stone or something and throw it at it and things like this. Now that made them the most intelligent thing in the world because no mammoth could come along and throw a stone at you, you know, and they learnt how to get milk out of goats, which I will tell you more about when I get on. But this is how they developed. The reason they developed so well was because their brains sort of developed with them, if you get what I mean. And this is the end of this lecture and thank you very much.

There's no doubt here: this is a case of setting out your theory *in extenso*. This is no weary rehash of information he's been given, but a new construction, undertaken in a spirit of intellectual excitement that comes through even in the transcript. There is no need for us to trace in detail what is happening to his knowledge. He is learning as he speaks, hypothesising, deriving new knowledge from the old. (One example of the way he sees the potentialities in his own formulations: 'making use of the things around it' is first introduced, without great emphasis, as one characteristic of the new ape-man, but is then recognised for its significance and becomes *the* central distinguishing idea about man, under which other features — killing animals for food, wearing skins, throwing stones — are now subsumed as *examples*.)

Nor is the value of this process placed in doubt because at the moment some of his ideas are wrong or inadequately informed. (Man's ancestor wasn't a four-legged ground dweller but a tree-dweller; the move to the ground *and* the change of diet were occasioned by the disappearance of the forests.) Because the theory is being made explicit and hypotheses derived from it, its errors are out in the open. They will immediately draw attention to themselves when conflicting 'correct' information comes along — and we may be sure he'll be on the look-out for anything at all that bears on his theory. Knowledge on the other hand which remains shadowy, unarticulated and unused can neither be definitely confirmed nor definitely invalidated. The uttering of error may have been avoided: but that is only because the error-generating potential of the ideas has remained latent — it hasn't gone away. We can learn from error, but not from confusion.

Let's concentrate on the other part of our enquiry: the way the enterprise is sustained.

It's clear that such an ambitious organising and extending of one's knowledge will not take place without some powerful commitment — if only because it's very hard work. The struggles to articulate, the long pauses, the gropings for words which we hear on the tape make this clear: no one is going to put themselves through that without strong motivation. This is not the sort of gentle assimilating process we are all aware of in day-dreaming and in the thinking we do as we drive the car. Moreover, Trevor has to do for himself what Terry and Robert did for each other.

Their dialogue kept going partly because each sensed discrepancies between his own and the other's knowledge and they forced each other to spell out implications and articulate assumptions. (Robert, it is true, sometimes responds as well to his *own* statements, sensing problems in them, and himself providing the explication his interlocutor might have demanded.) But Trevor has to keep going entirely on his own, probing his own knowledge and questioning his own formulations. What we need to get at is how, under what circumstances, children find the commitment to perform this probing and questioning for themselves.

One circumstance we've already mentioned, which is common to the examples we've considered, is the absence of formal constraints on the language. Expressive language such as they use (Trevor included) is loosely-structured, tolerant of false starts, changes of direction and loose ends, and communicates the feelings and responses of the speaker as well as his ideas. It is in some ways close to the language of conversation though it is stretched and strained more than that language normally is.

Next, all these utterances which we've been looking at as articulated thought, and which we've taken to represent intellectual steps forward for the speaker, have of course been produced with the ostensible purpose of communicating with and informing *someone else*. The points made in the discussions were definitely directed at the other participants. (Trevor's audience is at one remove, in that this is only a draft of what he will say to them, but that they are a real factor in his utterances is shown by the way he sometimes addresses them directly.) They all speak in the knowledge that they have a friendly, interested and tolerant audience.

We can see how necessary this knowledge must have been in Trevor's case. The task he is undertaking is a difficult one and will involve him in visibly struggling to express himself and sometimes in failing to make himself clear: he is given the confidence to proceed nevertheless by his knowledge of his listeners. They don't understand the development of man as he does and will be interested to listen to him. He will be able to speak to them as an expert to laymen. If he had to speak before, say, an examiner, he might be inhibited from being adventurous and taking risks in what he attempted.

It may also be that Trevor is helped in keeping up his flow of explication and elaboration by being able to envisage his audience's reactions to the points he is making. Perhaps he makes his statements more explicit by imagining the questions his audience would like to ask him. If his 'internalised audience' works like this, then it will again be important *what sort* of audience he sees it as.

Lastly, in all the examples we have looked at, the communication has been, so to speak, genuine. There has been a real reason for saying everything that has been said. The speakers have made available to their listeners ideas, views and responses which were available only from them, which they felt to be original and valuable and which (as they thought) their listeners would be glad to hear. (We might notice in passing that this is a different context of communication from the one common in schools in which the pupil writes down for the teacher things that the teacher already knows better than he does – an odd situation for the child, and one unlikely to encourage expansive articulation).

But that the speaker has something worth saying to say is not just an additional feature of these speculative learning processes but is the very thing we are trying to explain: the problem is, precisely, in what circumstances do children *have* something to say?

The conditions we've mentioned are clearly important – though they obviously can't explain *why* children undertake such strenuous probings of their knowledge. We've picked out the availability of a flexible expressive language; the sense of a sympathetic and interested audience; the genuiness of the communication as a transaction in a social situation – someone who wants to speak speaking to someone who wants to listen. The absence of any of these is likely to be at least an inhibiting factor – and the more inhibiting the less confident the speaker or writer: so that we may put children off committing themselves to words if for instance we frown on the informality of their expressive language or prescribe a particular form for their discourse. In other words if we want the water to flow we must keep the channels open. But what if it hasn't rained for a month?

Suppose we scan the material again for clues as to the sources of the commitment they all display. What about interest in the topic? Robert and Terry didn't choose their topic and probably weren't very interested in it to start with. But they became interested and really put their best efforts into trying to understand — the workings of water in porous rock. Why should they care about that of all things? Maybe the topic isn't as arid as it appears: Robert seems actually to be attracted by the processes he's contemplating: and indeed, the idea of water pushing a great big gigantic hole in the rock and then streaming down is exciting, and the way water 'goes up to the top' if you dip a sponge in it is something we all like to watch when it happens in front of us. Nor is Terry neutral in his attitude to caves and underground streams. They seem to hit on these good things as they talk and as a result become more committed to the topic. But they also seem to be driven by the discomfort of sensing inconsistencies in their two views of 'how it is' and a pleasure in working out 'how it must be'. Dialogue once under way may, it appears, become a self-motivating activity — though it will be powerfully fed if it touches potent symbolic material like caves.

Trevor was awestruck by the scale and scope and slowness of human progress and the incredibility of the idea that small things like taking shelter and skinning rabbits represent great irreversible advances. There's no doubt the topic was what excited him.

But the climate of India seems even less of a guaranteed winner than porosity, yet here are two twelve year old boys of so-called average ability seriously speculating about it, without adult instigation, in a South London comprehensive school. Their seriousness is that of craftsmen who want to make their artefacts as good as they can be and can only do it by organising and examining their knowledge. So it seems pupils may *become* involved in getting at the truth while pursuing some quite different purpose — such as making a good story.

Commitment, then, isn't a simple affair. There may be a strong interest in the topic, but it needn't be there initially — it can develop as the talking or writing proceeds. Moreover, interests, initial or otherwise, can arise from very diverse sources, and different children may be interested in the same thing for different reasons, any of which may suffice to draw them into the sort of efforts in language which lead them to fuller understanding.

Whatever the source of the involvement, we now return to the medium of its realisation. Most of this paper has been about talk: we've suggested that in talk children can go over their knowledge, look at it from different points of view, try it for size and kick it around; and that they often *need* to do this. We've looked at dialogue and spoken monologue as possible vehicles. When we now consider writing as a further possibility we must be struck by the fact that in most school contexts this vehicle is usually driven in completely different directions from the one we've been talking about. There is evidence* that it is typically seen not as a means of learning, but of recording information (for later reference or to fix it in the mind) and of showing the teacher how much has been learnt and understood. Yet what we've seen of the potentialities of extended monologue suggests that writing could be an important means of coming to grips with information and making sense of it.

If writing were to be used to such an end we would of course expect it to look very different from the 'subject writing' we're familiar with: in particular, if it is to allow the child to try out ideas he is not completely confident about, it will often have to provide a 'low-risk' situation free of the demand for a polished and final-looking performance, and so will, like talk, be likely to display features of looseness and informality and communicate a personal response to the topic; in other words, it will be expressive.

Examples of this sort of writing are not particularly easy to come by. (We'd like to receive more from teachers who are interested in getting in touch with us.) But we have two examples we'd like to quote, both by 13-year-olds, from the same history class but showing different sorts of possibilities. Both arose from a relationship with the teacher which allowed the children to be themselves without feeling they were on show (or on trial); both drew on an interest in the topic which had been created by good

* preliminary findings of the Writing Research

teaching.

Amanda was asked to write a Bolshevik political pamphlet. Instead she noted her *ideas* for such a pamphlet. It's interesting to speculate how far the expressive form her writing takes enables her to offer comments in a way that would not have been possible if she had carried out the task in the way she was asked to. The second example, which explains itself, is by *Trudi*.

Ideas for Pamphlet by Red Russians

1. *The war* Everyone, just about, wanted the war to end. This would be a good thing. We shall end the war, bring back the men etc. etc.

2. *The Czar* We would *definitely* get rid of the Czar once and for all whereas the Whites are more likely to let the Czar live and/or even bring him back to power. Restricted power, if they know what's good for them, to power.

3. *Bread* In stopping the war we would be more able to bring food to the cities. The trains would be free to bring what food there now is and the men would be coming back to farm the land again.

4. *The Land* The Whites said a piece of land for each man but we say the lands shall be owned by everyone so there would be no starving if you have a poor piece of land. *All* the land would belong to *all* the people.

5. *Power to the people* The power would belong to the people not the Czar or a Czar-orientated Government but to the people. The land would belong to the people governed by the people for the people.

6. *Work* Every technical advance will be used. The workers will have shorter days and better conditions because there is so much man-power, the advancement of machinery, especially in farming, has been very slow. The owners found it cheaper not to use expensive machines but we would be working not for profit but for the people.

7. *Join the army* They wanted men to join the army to fight the Whites. However, it would be very hard to get men who had just been fighting to join the army so they had to have some strong slogans like — if the Whites win they'll take your land away and send half of you to Siberia —

which wasn't true but it didn't matter if all you wanted was for men to join the army and they did.

What would you have done after Bloody Sunday if you had been the Czar? and what do you think the Czar did?

There were two ways the Czar could have taken:
1. to crush the rebellion by force
2. or to give the people civil rights

Myself I would have started having talks with representatives of the people to try and introduce civil rights although it would have been very difficult to pacify the people once they had been stirred. It would have been a lot easier if the people who came to the Square in front of the Winter Palace had not been fired upon. The changes would also have had to have been very fundamental which, if you and your family had had the supreme power that the Czar had had it would have been difficult to accept but anything would be better than war, civil war and disorder. One Council with representatives of the people, the army, the police, the secret police and the Crown would have had to have been introduced. Also a meet-the-people stint would have been a good idea. The whole family doing things the people did. Pictures of the princesses gardening, the Czarina cooking etc should have been dispatched. The Czar should have visited farms and mines and other places the people worked and even helped or had a go. The Czarina and the princesses should have visited the sick etc to show the people they were human. They should have stopped wearing so much finery. Maybe it wouldn't have worked but they should have tried. If they had visited the people and understood their conditions then they would have understood the people too.

The Czar I think the Czar's problem was he was too indecisive. He didn't take up a tough military plan to subdue the people or a rigid plan to get civil rights and understand the people. Instead he let it ride and panicked. He let others lead him and take the major decisions. He was also probably rather out of touch. If he had stood firm from the start either way, preferably civil rights, the results would have been better.

Both pieces are the result of an assignment set by the teacher. In the lesson which led up to the second piece, the teacher had broken off his account of the events at the crucial point: so the task he set simply provided an appropriate vehicle for the inevitable speculation. It involved taking what they knew and carrying it further, and also bringing in knowledge from other fields. (For instance, Trudi uses her knowledge of modern royalty's public relations procedures.)

The Bolshevik Pamphlet assignment asks for a construction, an imitation of a persuasive document. Writing it would involve taking the information you have and shaping it from a particular perspective and for a particular purpose. It would also involve bringing in your own wisdom about how people are persuaded. It is an invitation to take satisfaction from shaping a product, and the deploying of information would occur in the course of it. Amanda perhaps doesn't need this *extrinsic* reason for going over what she knows: she is interested less in the actual rhetorical construction and more in what ideas the Bolsheviks would present and why: and the loose form she chooses enables her to comment on the 'why'.

Of all the examples we have looked at — spoken and written — only the boys talking about porous rock and Trevor on the development of man can really be said to be 'rebuilding their theories' in a comprehensive and thoroughgoing way. The others certainly are making something of their knowledge by bringing it to bear on particular problems and are thereby making it real for themselves and getting inside it, but it's a gentler process. They aren't grappling with the information face to face to make sense of it, and discover what it amounts to, and see where they stand in relation to it. But then, not all information presents the sort of problems that call for this treatment. It seems that information which is abstract and difficult to comprehend, or which touches on powerful themes and deep concerns, or which is in some idiosyncratic way personally relevant to the learner, involves the person more completely in coming to terms with it. (Not that we can really claim to understand what makes a child go at it so wholeheartedly.) But if those are special cases, what is very often true is that information that comes to us from secondary experience — from teachers, books and so on — needs to be lived through and felt on the pulses in order to be truly known. If this is so it may be achieved, as we've seen, by building some construct which need not be primarily informative in function, or simply by talking, or writing about it in your own voice and with the same expressive modulations with which you speak of your own experience.

In all the examples the child has done something with his knowledge because he has wanted to — though what he has done may not be what he started by wanting. In some form or other he has taken action himself.

When the child doesn't particularly want to take action, that's the rainless situation we referred to earlier. But the drought may be of our own making, and the solution may, paradoxically, lie in attention to the channels. In other words it may be because we have kept too tight a control over the talking and writing that some children have ceased to use them for their own purposes of establishing personal relevances in the information they have come across and relating new experience to their total picture of the world. But if talk has a regular and *valued* place in the classroom and its agenda is wide open, and if the talking and writing are of the sort that enable the children to conduct their own *unsystematic* explorations without fear of censure and to communicate what they most have to say when they want to say it; then the themes and ideas that, differently for different individuals, have a potential for calling up their deep concerns and interests and thereby motivating committed enquiry, stand a good chance of being hit upon frequently; and when that happens, the means by which what demands to be done may be done will be there to hand and in good working order.

Why Write?

Nancy Martin, Peter Medway, Harold Smith, and Pat D'Arcy

Why Write? *is our second discussion pamphlet—and our second attempt to relate the theoretical ideas of the Writing Research to the objectives of the different areas of the curriculum.*

The Theory

The theory provides a model which does not simply *list* the different kinds of writing but makes clear the relationships between them; it has specific things to say about the development of writing abilities, about what comes before what, and why; it relates the different sorts of writing to the mental processes (learning, creativity, reasoning etc) which the teacher is concerned to foster; it provides a basis for a consistent approach to language in all parts of the curriculum, in particular giving the 'English' component an intelligible place in the whole rather than treating it as if it were an entirely different species.

As teachers we are interested not in the development of writers as writers, but in writing as a means of development—cognitive, affective and social. That writing may be such a means is due to the nature of its two faces: on the one hand it looks to other people and seeks to transfer something to them by way of informing, advising, commanding, persuading and sharing; on the other, it can also organise more clearly for the writer himself whatever perceptions he has about the world he lives in and his own relation to it. Using this second face enables him to select and hold for closer contemplation aspects of his own experience which can be scanned for particular features—sorted into logical or chronological order, rearranged for his own satisfaction, invested with particular feelings and so on. This process of personal selection, contemplation and differentiation is very important, because it *changes the writer*, he is a different person when he has done it, because now he has articulated a feeling or a thought or an attitude more clearly, or seen how a bit of his experience fits into the pattern which he is gradually building up for himself; in other words, he is more conscious than he was. It is these processes which can go on in writing which can make it so powerful in an educational sense.

But in encouraging them to happen we must also take into account the other face of the writer which seeks an audience outside himself, because most voluntary writing is motivated by this sense of communication.

About this Pamphlet

So these papers are concerned with the ways in which writing changes under the influence of who it is for and what it is doing. We have attempted to describe the major kinds of writing and to illustrate the way some children have used them in their early years in the secondary school. Because we have tried to catch learning on the wing, as it were, some of the examples may, at first sight, seem alarmingly imperfect: we hope readers will understand that these examples are not seen as models of good writing but as an attempt to document children's writing in transition as part of a *learning process*.

Because we now know that many teachers associated with the Project have found this theory useful in a variety of situations across the whole curriculum, we have put together in this pamphlet new versions of the theoretical papers which they originally received, revised to include examples of some of the kinds of writing which came from schools where the teachers were familiar with our theory. We hope that in this form it will be useful to both primary and secondary teachers whatever their particular 'subject' interests happen to be.

1. *A Sense of Audience: The Child and His Reader*

A sense of audience—how the writer pictures his reader—although very obviously important when we consider the range of adult writing, may not at first sight seem so relevant to school writing since almost all of it is produced for one sort of reader—the teacher. But in fact the notion of Audience has powerful implications for school writing and in this section we try briefly to explain why.

It is true that children in school write mostly for the teacher. But what makes for differences between the pieces of writing is not, objectively, who the reader is, but how the writer *sees* his reader; and children see their teachers in very different ways. Not only may different children's views of the same teacher vary, but a child may see his teacher as a different sort of reader on different occasions.

In differentiating the sorts of 'Sense of Audience' that we find in school writing, we have found these categories (which the earlier Writing Research team formulated) very useful:

    Child (or adolescent) to Self
    Child (or adolescent) to Trusted Adult
    Pupil to Teacher as Partner in Dialogue
    Pupil to Teacher, Particular Relationship
    Pupil to Teacher seen as Examiner or Assessor
    Writer to his Readers (or his Public)

'Child to Self' writing is writing which takes no account of the needs of a reader other than oneself—as in some diaries, notes and first drafts. By contrast, writing for a Public Audience is capable of being read and understood by a complete stranger, so most published writing comes in this category, as does some school writing (particularly stories) by older students.

Writing for a teacher could come under any of the middle four categories. In 'Child to Trusted Adult', a personal relationship seems more relevant than the pedagogic one, and the writing occurs because there is this particular person who will respond sympathetically; so the child may write about personal or deeply felt matters such as he would not venture upon if he did not feel very secure with his reader. 'Pupil to Teacher as Partner in Dialogue' covers writing which is recognisably part of an educational process: the child still feels secure in the teacher's presence and is assuming that the teacher is there to help him and will be interested in what he is saying. Where there is a 'Particular Relationship' with a particular teacher, the child may risk being honest, tentative and frank as in the 'Child to Trusted Adult' situation, the only difference being that the subject matter relates specifically to the *educational* setting, rather than, for instance, to the child's family life. It is comparable with an 'apprentice to master' relationship. 'Pupil to Teacher seen as Examiner or Assessor' refers not only to exams but to all writing which the child appears to be producing merely to satisfy a teacher's demand and on which he is expecting to be judged or assessed—either for how well he has written or for what he has shown he knows.

Far from being confined to examinations and formal tests, writing for the 'Examiner' audience accounted, in a 1966 sample from 65 secondary schools, for about half of all school writing. Even in the first year it was 40%.*

In other words, in schools—institutes of learning—the single most important use for writing appears to be as a means of testing, of monitoring knowledge and performance. This writing is seen not as *part* of the learning process but as something which happens *after* the learning.

In the belief that writing could actually be part of learning, and in particular could be an important means whereby children might get into new fields and unfamiliar ideas and begin to understand them, we have been working with teachers on ways of making writing into something children feel they can *use*. We felt strongly that the 'Examiner audience' situation inhibited thinking and speculation and that the child needed what he wrote to be read with interest and sympathy rather than to be judged as the performance of a task.

The writing which follows resulted from situations in which teachers were willing to accept and even to encourage a 'Trusted Adult' situation in which the writer felt free to 'come out' with his thoughts in writing as he might more often do in speech.

---

* Preliminary findings from the Schools Council Project: The Development of the Written Language of 11-18 year olds.

Writing (A) resulted from an experimental approach by one teacher along these lines. The subject was Social Studies, the school a multi-racial boys' comprehensive and the course was a new one. The teacher asked the boys to keep a log in which they could say anything they wanted to say about the work. He decided before they started that his response would be that of a partner in the same enterprise: he *was* an adult and a teacher, and this would be acknowledged, but he would not mark or evaluate the logs, instead he would write back.

(A) LM 6.9.72

> I don't like being told what to do, I like doing things what I like doing not what others want me to do. I am not interest in any other lessons, I don't thing my mum and dad were very interest in lessons at school. I don't thing about leaving school, I feel that the day I leave school in two years time seems a long way a way, but looking on the last two years it has gone very quick, two quick not to thing about leaving. I moan to much to my sisters and my mates sometimes I even moan to my mum and dad. I am a shy person with my relatives but not with my mates. I say things with my mates, but not to my relatives, and my relatives are not what you call angels, more comes out when I talk to somebody who's not my relative.

Teacher 12.9.72

> You have made a very good explanation of the kind of person you are. When you have examined what the development of man has been like, perhaps you will understand yourself better.
>
> Most people of your age go through the confusion you have described. It is important that you are aware of yourself because it will help you leave these doubts and confusions behind.
>
> Although it is right to be independent and only do what you want you should remember you can learn a lot from other people and by reading, studying and thinking.
>
> You should start your work on prehistory as soon as possible

LM 13.9.72

Today I wrote about the Erect-man. When I first started I wasn't interested. When I started getting invold with writing about it, I began to enjoy doing writing the Erect-man.

Teacher 18.9.72

Write in your log book how much you understood about the development of your own body by studying Homo erectus. Always write your personal reaction to what you are finding out. You have made a good start.

Would you mind also explaining in the log what brought on your bad mood yesterday, why you left early, why you were stroppy, what you think of the group and what you think about our new school Council representative.

LM undated

Yesterday when I came into the group in a bad mood was because I was fed up with school that day. When I get fed up, I always get in a bad temper and then I swear to much. Then people get a bad impression of me. The group is alright and should be alright. But I think it should have been Nobby D-- doing our group reproestive again this year.

SL 6.9.72

Today I we not sure of what to do or what some of the things meant I didn't know what things like civilisation meant. Then I got bored and started larking because all in all it wasn't an exactly working day.

Teacher 12.9.72

Understanding what civilisation means will come to you as the course goes along. In the meantime look it up in the dictionary.

'Getting bored' means losing your concentration. Concentraion is making an effort to think.

SL 13.9.72

I really think you are right when you said I don't understood about civilisation because I don't but I'm sure it'll come to me as you said I was bored because I wasn't interested in the work it wasn't interested I didn't understand. I will read think about it until I understand it then I'll write.

SL 13.9.72

Today I think I learned a little bit about prehistory today I learned about the Handy Man. I learned about Dr Leakey who probably lived with ape men I liked today's lesson But I don't think I done enough for four lessons I spent a long time reading thats probably why

Teacher 13.9.72

You haven't done much as you said but your explanation in your log book was excellent.

SL undated

This was probably my best day of all I understood it all and got through more work than any other lesson.

Writing (B) happened because the teacher suggested that two boys might like to act as reporters about an experimental situation in woodwork. Instead of each boy concentrating on his own product the woodwork area was turned into a 'factory' for the day and all the work was organised like an assembly line. Although the full account is in print elsewhere we have chosen to use the opening two paragraphs from Francis's account here, because it seems to us to demonstrate very clearly the freedom of expression which can occur when the teacher is in a 'Trusted Adult' rather than a more teacher-like role—though, in this case, there was also the influence of an audience of other children since Francis's report was intended to be presented to his own class. The knowledge that an audience will be a peer-group can powerfully affect the way children write. After all, they *know* what this audience will be interested in.

Why Write? 41

(B) *Report by Francis Cleary*

	(Class) S.1.C and S.1.E today are making tables for the old people which is a very good cause: Another thing about this work is that it is all
series	volinteerly. There is a serrious of jobs for different people. This room is termendosly changed, in the way that there is no time for talking all
serious	searosery work. Ordinary days is nowhere near in this room today. People comes from room to room as they please. The people has not spiritly changed but mently changed. The lasy people are bissy and bissy people are bissyer still. Mister Comer is changed a lot in no bad way ither. Any other day it would be do what you are told to do and no wandrowing about. Today it is do as you please, wander as you please as long as it has to do with the job. People is exchanging jobs which is unusall for this room espically when Mister Comer is in it.
complicated	all this work is complated but it is a break for all the boys the break is to show what kind of a worker he is. In this room there are some very good workers like Paddy McDonald, Antony Teggart and Patsy Doran. Then there are some poor workers like Tomas McMegoire who is just not trying his best.
	Having changed rooms I can see that room or rather the people are working very differently. Different jobs again are done by different people. The jobs in this room is not as difficult as the jobs in the other room. The teacher again is changed from ordinary in the way that he is not as bosey althought he is bosey a little. I think looking and listing to bouth teachers I think I would rather have Mister Comer in a lot of ways. About five yards away from where I am the first table is almost finished and from this I can say that it is going to be very nice and
observer	so does my other fellow observe that is along with me he also thinks that it is a little shakie

boys	but I disagree with him there in every way posible about this table anyway. Laim McCullough is the fourman and is over all the boy involved in this job. I think that he should not have been foorman in fact he should not have been included in the job because he does not work this might be because he thinks he is the
bossing	big man when he is fourman an bousing the boys about which he does not do. Some people showes that they do not like Laim by calling him, slave-driver and big head and say that they would like to kill him and through him out the window. I do not like Laim becaus when I asked him some questions he was not very
cooperative	(coropited) coriprable and because he will not help the people he does not like but he is allways helping the people he likes very well.

2. *Functions of Writing*

In Paper 1 we looked at the effect on a writer of who he is writing for. In this Paper we shall be looking at another major influence on a writer—his sense of *what* it is for. This is not exactly the same as his purpose because our culture has itself developed distinct language forms which are typically associated with certain situations. We know quite well, for instance, when we are in a story, or a sermon, or being persuaded to buy something—because we have internalised these kinds of language from our day-to-day encounters with them. When children come to write in similar situations they draw on their pool of language experience which helps them to know what kind of language to use in certain types of situation. For instance, no-one teaches children in an infant class to begin their stories 'Once upon a time', or 'Once there was a little pig . . .' but most of them do this because this beginning is so obviously a 'marker' of stories which they have listened to or read.

The boundaries are by no means hard and fast but it has been found possible and useful to distinguish three broad categories of function to which recognisably distinct kinds of writing belong. What distinguishes them is that writer and reader mutually recognise the conventions that distinguish one 'job' from another. It is true that there are often linguistic differences but these are the markers of the different functions whose essential difference lies in the sort of things the writer takes for granted about his reader's responses. To take a simple example, if we read 'Once upon a time there was a flying horse' we know the writer is taking it for granted that we recognise a story and shall not quarrel about whether horses can fly.

The three 'recognised and allowed for' functions of writing which can be distinguished in the language are these:—

Expressive: *in which it is taken for granted* that the writer himself is of interest to the reader; he feels free to jump from facts to speculations to personal anecdote to emotional outburst and none of it will be taken down and used against him—it is all part of being a person vis à vis another person. It is the means by which the new is tentatively explored, thoughts may be half-uttered, attitudes half-expressed, the rest being left to be picked up by a listener or reader who is willing to take the unexpressed on trust.

The following excerpt from a long account of a project in metal-work by a boy of twelve illustrates many of the features of expressive writing.

> *The becoming of gnat killer*
> the name Gnat Killer came to me after the project for maths I had been doing, you see I was going to do a project to see how many people spelt Gnat rong they ither spell it Kat, Gnate, Knate, Knatte, and even Knatt. well when I started to do my project, I thought well I will call it the Gnat then Killer came into my mind because I am mad on Horror. So I called it the Gnat Killer, it may sound violent but it isn't well at least I don't think, it is only another name been created to the world for the perpose of a project, I dont thoe if my turnin two the dictionary, it will read
>
> Gnat Killer
> name for

>   a dagger used
>   by Ricky Baker
>   in 1972 8th dec:
>   (not spelt nat killer)
>   in italics:
> that is only my idear thoe not that it will work.

Clearly this writing is very like written down speech, reflecting the ebb and flow of the writer's thoughts and feelings—and this is what expressive language (spoken or written) does. But speech is always on the move: it moves according to the demands of what it is for, what the listener wants to hear, and how the speaker's language resources allow him to meet these demands—his own and other people's. So expressive speech shuttles to and fro in opposite directions, and expressive writing can be seen to move in a similar way, either towards the *Transactional* or towards the *Poetic*.

Transactional: *in which it is taken for granted* that the writer means what he says and can be challenged for its truthfulness to public knowledge, and its logicality; that it claims to be able to stand on its own and does not derive its validity from coming from a particular person. So it is the typical language of science and of intellectual inquiry, of technology, of trade, of planning, reporting, instructing, informing, advising, persuading, arguing and theorising—and, of course, the language most used in school writing.

Ian was in the same metal-work class as Ricky. His project was a brass dish and he wrote a long piece about brass and how you work it and how he made his dish; but, although there are many expressive features in his writing, his purpose is firmly transactional. He feels himself to be knowledgeable about brass and sets out to *inform* his readers. The differences between his piece and Ricky's (quoted above) illustrate the differences between writing that is focussed on a transaction and writing following the free flow of the writer's thoughts and feelings.

> *About Brass*
>
> Brass is an yellow alloy of copper and zinc in varying proprotions with quantities of lead tin and iron brass is very

malleable, fusible ductile and readilly cast and machined, Muntz or yellow metal is a variety of brass containing 60% copper, As it resists corrosion well, it is largely used for ship propellors, bows and fittings, corrosion means rusting away.

Some examples of what brass can make:
1) electrical fixtures
2) unexpensive jewelry
3) metal decorations
4) table lighter
5) trombone
6) screws
7) marine hardware

A percentage table
copper	60%
brass	37%
white alloy	3%
	100%

In the famous Praha football stadium, nearly everything in side the walls are made out of copper including the goalpost, the team that play here are Sparta Prague. Mallable means easy to work with, and very dicible.

Poetic: *in which it is taken for granted* that 'true or false?' is not a relevant question at the literal level. What is presented may or may not in fact be a representation of actual reality but the writer takes it for granted that his reader will *experience* what is presented rather in the way he experiences his own memories, and not *use* it like a guidebook or map in his dealings with the world— that is to say, the language is not being used instrumentally as a means of achieving something, but as an end in itself. When Huck Finn said all Tom Sawyer's great stories were lies he was mistaking the function of stories (the poetic function) and operating the 'rules' of the other 'game'—the transactional. So a reader *does* different things with transactional and poetic writings: he uses transactional writing, or any bit of it, for any purpose, but who can say what we 'do' with a story or a poem that we read, or a play we watch? Perhaps we just share it with the writer; and not having to 'do' anything with it leaves us free to attend to its formal features—which are not explicit—the pattern of events in a narrative, the configuration of an idea and, above all, the pattern of feelings evoked: in attending in this non-instrumental way we experience feelings and values as part of what we are sharing. Writing in the poetic function shows a heightened awareness of symbolic, aural and even visual qualities—of shaping a verbal construct; for instance seven-year-old children begin their stories in the way their experience has taught them—'Once there was a little giraffe . . . '—and they often write 'The End' on a separate line as conclusion. Older children, of course, shape their writing in the poetic function in more sophisticated ways (see the anonymous story in Paper 5, 'Growth from the Expressive'), and we include here a poem by Timothy, aged 12.

> *The Arabs*
> Hurtling across the sand
> On their white horses
> Robes flowing behind
> like madmen they charge
> Seemingly never to cease
> The Horses' hooves pound on the
> scorched sand of the desert
> Their scimatars flashing in the sun
> They mount a dune
> Pause
> Then they are away
> Vanishing into the distant sands.

How the Three Functions Are Related

Our theory, then, describes three functions to be found in our language and goes on to describe the relationship between them. The expressive is basic: its equivalent in speech is the vehicle of the great bulk of communications between mankind. The transactional and the poetic are best seen as developments from the expressive to meet more specialised requirements. For instance, both the expressive and the transactional may convey information, but in the transactional the writer's personal attitude to the information may be suppressed as being irrelevant to what the reader needs to know. The reader is assumed to want to *use* the information, so in writing to your Insurance Company to tell them you have changed your car, you don't say how attached you were to your old one; writing to your mother you do.

Similarly, both the expressive and the poetic may recount a narrative, but in the transactional this is subservient to some other end—for information, or as an illustration—whereas in the poetic the focus is on the shaping of the tale, on the selection and ordering of the pattern of events and characters and contexts so that the story may stand on its own to be experiences as an end in itself.

3. Genuine Communication

The two models of 'Function' and 'A Sense of Audience' make it possible for us to look at the range of writing which children are doing in all their school work; and it allows us to be quite precise about the development of their ability to write appropriately for different purposes and different audiences.

Development is to a large extent a process of specialisation and differentiation: we start by writing the way we talk to each other—expressively, and envisaging as our reader a single, real, known person; gradually we may acquire, *in addition*, the capacity to use the transactional and the poetic, and to write for an unspecified, generalised or unknown audience. Further this differentiation ideally occurs as a result of coming to hold those adult purposes for which the mature forms of writing have been evolved, and of learning to anticipate the needs of different and remoter audiences. So the development of writing abilities is partly conditional on the more general development of the child out of egocentrism; but that general development may itself be aided by the practice of writing.

Writing (like talk) organises our picture of reality, and, at the same time and by the same process communicates it to someone else. It is true that for educational purposes the first is more relevant than the second: we ask children to write so that they will organise their world picture, not so that we can learn things from them. But it is a fact of life that we can't have one without the other. Language *has* two faces and we are well advised to take account of both. The moral we draw from this is that, if we want writing to be a means of thinking and of active organising, we must make sure that the writer feels he has a genuine communication to make and is not merely performing an exercise—which was how David, aged thirteen, saw it: he said, 'You write it down just to show the teacher that you've done it, but it doesn't bring out any more knowledge in you'.

'Genuine communication' for a child, in whatever context—writing for history, English, science, a letter, a diary—is very often going to mean an inseparable blend of giving an account of the topic and expressing a response to it. If this is so, we should accept the mixture; if we discourage the personal element in it, we risk making writing an unwieldy and alien instrument instead of a natural extension of the child's own mental processes. And accepting it means more than simply allowing it to happen: it means agreeing to be communicated with in that way and making ourselves a real audience to a child by giving an authentic response to the communication as a communication rather than by giving back an evaluation of how well he has accomplished the task.

The child's early writing is necessarily expressive because he has not yet come to differentiate his purposes nor appreciate the differing needs of differing audiences. But the mixture of thinking and feeling, subjective and objective, personal and public, which we find in the child's expressive language is characteristic of our mental processes too—of the way we think and react—and this is so at all stages, and not only when we are young. This would suggest that the expressive ought to continue to be an important vehicle for, say, assimilating new ideas encountered in school, even after the child has learned to use the transactional and the poetic. In that case, the need will probably persist for an audience which is seen as sympathetic and non-evaluative and in whose presence the child feels he can, as it were, talk to himself—think aloud (see the examples quoted in Paper 1 above). The professional scientist writes in the transactional for publication but may do part of his thinking in expressive letters to friends: we need to provide both social situations for children (and, of course, not only in science).

Many children never come to be at home in the transactional. Too often they perform a sort of empty mimicry of the style of the adult academic writing they have met—in text books and elsewhere—without the transactional ever becoming the natural vehicle for setting out information and ideas for specific purposes. Our theory suggests that we might do better by devising situations in which, for instance, 'informative' writing has a genuine informative function—someone is going to use the information and provide feedback as to its usefulness, making it clear what is and is not relevant to his needs. Children are commonly asked to write down information for a teacher who, they are well aware, knows it better than they do. Often there is the additional fiction that the reader is not the teacher (which he patently is!) but some vaguely perceived public audience. Of course, exposure to adult models of good transactional writing will be important: but children will naturally take from the models at each stage whatever fulfils a felt need; this is a far cry from the docile imitation of style and tone which produces so much lifeless posturing in school writing.

The poetic, too, might be expected to develop readily out of the expressive—and not only in English lessons, if children have been encouraged to use the expressive mode of writing in other subject areas. The desire to shape writing, in which there is a strong personal investment and an increasing awareness of the potential of language as a creative medium, should grow naturally out of lively, involved expressive writing. It is not a question here of informing, or organising or even persuading a given audience, but rather of presenting for them an experience which has been transformed from the anecdotal, rather informal 'chat' level into a construct which can be shared, enjoyed and appreciated by a wider audience.

So what is necessary is for the child to be put into situations which are so constructed that he feels a genuine need to operate in a particular way. This is explored in greater detail in Paper 4.

4. Single Situations Not Kinds of Writing

A teacher in one of our associated schools wrote to us asking, 'Should children be taught to distinguish between the three types of writing?' (expressive, transactional and poetic).

In our view this would not be helpful—quite the reverse—but we do think that if children understand that what they write needs to be different for different purposes and audiences they could set about writing with more confidence, and confidence is a major element in developing writing.

In real life every writing situation is different; even in the case of a journalist writing for a particular paper with a stable readership, or a secretary of a committee writing reports of meetings—to take two examples where the situations at first sight might appear to repeat themselves—a good writer would in each case be aware of differences in the circumstances from other occasions and would reflect these in his reports. So it would be helpful for children to understand this potential diversity of writing, and our advice would be to *set up situations* for writing with clearly stated purposes and varied audiences, real or imaginary, to work from occasion to occasion and to let a sense of the functions of writing develop through experience of writing for a variety of audiences and purposes. Until children are actually operating writing in different modes (or functions) they can't see the differences; all they will see will be different surface features, such as the convention of not using 'I' in science reports. In practice there is no reason why the first person should not be used, particularly in the early years of learning science, since the separation of the doer from what he does is a sophisticated mental activity and may prevent assimilation of new knowledge and reflection on it.

But for most children it is not enough just to set up a situation by stating an audience and a purpose. They need to enter into the whole situation, and here we should like to explore a little more fully what 'entering into a whole situation' might mean. Everyone does this without conscious effort in speech. Our relationships and attitude to whoever we are speaking to, and to what we are talking about, and to the total situation (which may cause us to feel shy, confident, relaxed, frightened etc) is reflected in the way we speak on these different occasions because we are part of a real situation: we know who we are talking to, or we know we don't know them and our speech changes accordingly. In school writing the situation is either that it is a task done directly for the teacher, or the children are asked to enter into an imaginary situation, for example, 'Life for me as a peasant', 'A letter from a worker in a tea-garden in Ceylon', or 'An eye-witness account of one of the miracles of Jesus'.

In both these writing situations—the real and the imaginary—we think the teachers of all subjects could help their pupils by discussing with them what a particular piece of writing is for, and who it is for—the teacher? the writer? (with the teacher as an interested background audience) the class? And is the writing to show what the pupil knows? or to explore ideas for himself? or to share his ideas with someone else?

When the situation is an imaginary one, as in the examples quoted above, we think that deliberate steps need to be taken to help the children enter into the whole situation before they write. It is quite a feat of imagination to cast oneself in roles other than one's own, so it often happens that children have a kind of split focus in these situations, and what dominates is the sense that this is only a game and what is really wanted is for them to get into their piece the things they have learned about in the lesson, and this operates against their drawing on their own experience of life to envisage the attitudes, feelings and possible actions that could be part of the imaginary situation. For instance, children could write powerfully about being a peasant because they themselves are subject to authority in a way adults are not; moreover many of them are small people physically compared to adults. From such a starting link between the imagined character and themselves they can then select from the information of the history lesson to put flesh on the bones of their daily lives as a peasant which they know is different in detail from their own.

If when setting up these imaginary situations teachers could spend a little time in talking with the children about the situation and in getting the children to envisage verbally, or by dramatic improvisation, how these imaginary people might think, feel and act, we think the children would step more completely and confidently into the roles they are being asked to play in times past or places distant. We also think that if all teachers who set written work discussed these kinds of questions with the children—over a period of time—they would be helped to become aware of the diversity of writing that is possible, and would learn to take up the needs of different situations in the way they already do in speech.

The really important thing about writing is to keep one's *main attention* focussed on what one wants to say and on netting this in words. At the same time, however, one's *subsidiary attention* is concerned with the physical task of using a pen to get the words down on the page, and somewhere in the background, out of sight, out of mind most of the time, is the 'reader over one's shoulder' acting like a prompter to bring the mind and pen to rest on appropriate utterances. If one stops to think about the reader, or the words one is using, one's focal attention has momentarily changed places with one's subsidiary attention and one has to scan back in order to get focussed, once again, on whatever it is 'out there' that one is trying to capture in words. So if a child were asked to write, for instance, an 'expressive' piece or a 'transactional' piece, it would shift his attention from *what* he wants to say on to *how* he is to say it, and we think that attention on the *how* should have been focussed earlier by what went on before the writing began (the situation, the talk about it etc).

Being able to envisage an audience, and shape one's utterance to take account of that audience, is part of growing up. Young children tend to see everything through the filter of their own viewpoint, so discussion of who is actually going to read what they they write, or who they are to imagine will read it, may help children because it reminds them of the speaker-listener situation in speech which they have always known and where they have resources they can draw on.

5. Growth from the Expressive

TRANSACTIONAL ◄ ◄ ◄ EXPRESSIVE ► ► ► POETIC

In Paper 2 we said that expressive speech is the vehicle of the great bulk of communication between mankind. Expressive writing is a similar sort of 'matrix' out of which more specialised and differentiated kinds of writing can grow. In this paper we try to document stages in that growth towards differentiation—to catch on the wing the process of moving towards the greater explicitness of the transactional, or the more conscious shaping of the poetic.

We have chosen three pieces of writing for illustration and comment. The first is by James from St Paul's Secondary School, Bessbrook, Northern Ireland; the second by John, from Chelsea School, London; and the third by a girl who asked to remain anonymous—all aged twelve.

JAMES

James was asked to record his thoughts during a silent 'sit-in'.

> I am thinking that when I go home I wont have to do any sticks and I hope my friend will come out right away. When I call up for him he says wait for a moment and he does be an hour. When you go home there is lots of things to do. When you have no work to do you could play a game of football or even a game of tig.

This writing is expressive (as we have defined 'expressive' in Paper 2). It reflects James's thoughts and feelings and attitudes ('When I call up for him he says wait for a moment and he does be an hour'), even his uncertainties about what he is writing. The task he was set gave him little guidance as to what his 'reader' wanted or expected, so he wavers. There is a sign of his moving into a narrative—'he says wait for a moment and he does be an hour'—but immediately he abandons the embryo story—his move towards the poetic—and starts making generalisations about how to fill in time, which take him towards the transactional. The writing reflects the writer's uncertainties. He seems not to have felt the need either to inform his teacher in any detail of his thoughts and feelings (a transaction of communicating information) or to give his thoughts and feelings shape to satisfy himself (a direction towards the poetic).

JOHN

Our second example comes from John, who had been finding out about the area around his school, and on his return wrote this:

> After the war the Germans came over to Britain and built Fulham Gasworks. With it they built a square called the German square. Now it is called Imperial Square. In the Square there are gas lamps and they are still working. They still have gas in them. Some people said that the gasworks might be pulled down. All along Michael Road and Harwood Road the houses are going to be pulled down because they are going to build a flyover. The old lady in no. 9 Imperial Square said that she doesn't care if they are going to knock down the house because she has had her happy days and now she is old and she is no longer wanted. No one loves her. Her house has been standing for a hundred years. All the houses in Imperial Square have been standing up for a long time. The people there complain about the supporters come through Imperial Square and they smash bottles and other bad things. This lady said that when the Germans were there it was very hard to get a job. You had to get up very early to queue up to get a job in the power station. It must have been very hard for the people. They might have to wait about six hours before the gates open, then they might not still get a job. I would not like to been in those days. I bet their houses were running with rats. They had no food hardly, there clothes were dirty, they were dirty, they had diseases. It must have been terrible for them. I felt sorry for the lady who we was talking to. It must have been hard for her. People from everywhere came to the Gasworks to get a job. Where my friend lives, his name is Leslie, at the end of his street called Elb Street there is a place there, it has gas there, they put it in the lorries. That has been standing for about a

hundred years, and Langford School, that was built in 1889. I used to go there and my brothers went there. I like that school. I will remember that school. Lots of old ladies must have memories but if they tell you they might think that we think the things they are saying to us is silly. It is sad for some of the old people. Their husbands have died in the war and now they have no one to talk to. They are all alone but this is life. No one can live for ever. It's very sad. Where I live in Pearscroft Road there is a place called Bulow Court. Before that was built there was a road going through there called Bulow Road. There must be something done about these old people. I don't know what but something.

John had been given a much clearer idea of his task than James. There can be little doubt that he sees his role as informant and he begins firmly in this role, but as he gets under way he shifts from information to speculation and direct expression of his feelings about 'those days' and about the old lady who had informed him. ('It must have been very hard for the people . . . I would not like to been in those days . . . It must have been terrible for them. I felt sorry for the lady who we was talking to').

There are few signs of deliberate structuring. It is written all in one piece and he sees no reason to restrict himself to information—and why should he? His attitudes and feelings are as much a discovery as the locale and its inhabitants. The selection and ordering of his account seems to be determined by his feelings, and, as in all expressive writing, he takes it for granted that the information he wants to give will be what his reader wants to know.

What marks this piece out as a step towards a differentiated transactional function is the writer's clear conviction that he is presenting real information ('After the war the Germans came over to Britain and built Fulham Gas Works' and so on); it has therefore the stamp of a genuine communication.

A GIRL

The third piece we have selected for comment is no less firmly in the expressive. It is very near speech: it backtracks and slips into 'asides' and digresses to inform the reader about the game they were playing ('Now if you don't know what Hooky is, well I'll tell you it is a game that . . .'); but it also has other features which suggest that the writer had just as clear a sense that she was writing a *story*, albeit a real one, as John had a sense of presenting real information. Furthermore it must be remembered that this writer wished to be anonymous, so, although it was written for her teacher to read as 'first' audience, she must also have had a sense of some subsequent unknown audience in London. Writing for a wider unknown audience is one of the features that distinguishes differentiated writing and causes the writer to shape it more deliberately. In the shaping of her memories this writing is approaching story form.

The Secret

As I tried to hold back my tears of shame a vision of that awful game loomed before me. My mane problem was should I tell my mother or should I not. You see it all began one night when I had a friend staying with me or at least I thought she was a friend. Mum and Dad were out and my friend mentioned playing a game. As she told us about it I was frightened. This is what she told us. One night in the boarding school where she went to they played a game called 'Hooky' Now if you don't know what Hooky is, well I'll tell you it is a game that involves contacting the spirits and asking the spirit questions such as. What age will you get married at, will you do well in your exams, or anything else you wish to ask the spirit. She told us of one time when the spirit would not leave the room, and the girls had to get a blessed cross to get rid of the spirit. My friend nearly insisted on play-ing the game in our house, although I did not aprove my brother seemed to find no harm in doing so. I said nothing but stayed in the room as the game comenced. My friend thought she had got a spirit so she asked what age would she get married at no reply came so she asked again. The glass on the table moved to the letter B, that was the second letter of the Albhet which meant number two. Then the glass on the table moved to D, that was number four. She was to get married at twenty four. My friend asked my brother to ask it a question, my brother said that he didnt want to and that he didnt want to play anymore. So my friend asked the spirit to go, and to give some sign of when it is going. The spirit rattled the blinds as it left. I was scared stiff. But my friend just laughed. I was not going to tell Mum about it because I knew she would not abrove. The next day I decided to tell mum. I counted to five and then I told her. Mum didnt say much but she told me it was against the Catholic Religion to play this game. That was my secret told and it had lifted a great load from my head. And I went to confession vowing never again. And also not to assoiate very much with my friend again.

The ways in which this writer begins and ends are perhaps the most clearly deliberate and controlled features of her story. She does not plunge into the narrative but begins with a statement of her guilt and her problem—'Should I tell my mother or should I not'. Then follows the train of events which tumble out very much as they might in speech, and they give the impression that they are in control of her rather than she of them. But in the last few sentences she is in control again, and moves firmly into the last sentences of the actual narrative—'I counted five and then I told her. Mum didnt say much but she told me it was against the Catholic Religion to play this game'. The actual story is now ended but she does not end here; she moves into a wider context, just as she began from a wider context, and in her last sentence her language is a long way from speech—'I went to confession vowing never again. And also not to assoiate very much with my friend again'.

Although we may assume this is a true story, the form of all stories, whether true or invented, is shaped by the teller, and we suggest that this piece of writing is in transition towards the poetic.

It could, of course, be argued that her purpose in writing this piece was to inform, and in the sense that all writing implies an act of communication this is true, but her focus on shaping a series of events and emotions into a complete construct suggests that information is not her dominant purpose. As with all stories in the poetic function, hers is to be experienced rather than used.

We have chosen these examples of expressive writing in transition because we believe that differentiation from the matrix of expressive language is the process by which children learn, and also learn to write. We see learning and learning to write as linked, and capable of being more closely associated than they often are in practice. We also believe that the need for expressive language remains wherever there are new experiences to be assimilated and that the expressive is the continuing source from which specialised forms of language can grow.

To Sum Up

WE BELIEVE . . .

— that writing can serve a much wider purpose than it usually gets the opportunity to serve in schools.
— that talk and writing are closely related and that talk can arise out of writing just as writing can arise out of talk.
— that both talk and writing are valuable activities for *all* pupils to engage in at some time.
— that on each occasion there is a decision to be made as to whether talk or writing is more appropriate.
— that it is helpful to teachers in making such decisions for them to be able to see what other teachers have done in similar circumstances.
— that because of the pressures of his own timetable the individual teacher finds it very difficult to see what other teachers have done.
— that for the same reason it is difficult for the teacher to see research findings in the field of pupils' language (written and oral).
— that it would be worthwhile *to set up a network* which would enable teachers to exchange experiences, researchers to indicate research findings, and both to suggest new fields for inquiry.

more specifically:
— that a 'map' of different kinds of writing can be of value to teachers.

- that the map, produced by the Writing Research Unit at the London University Institute of Education, dealing with *'function'* and *'audience'*, could be of particular value to teachers.
- that these ideas, if they are to be valuable, need trying out in schools, where they can be applied, refined and extended.
- that it is desirable that more school writing should be in functions other than generalising or classificatory.
- that it is helpful to the pupil's learning if he gets the opportunity on occasions to choose his own way of handling a topic.
- that it is positively harmful to most pupils' learning if they have always to handle topics in somebody else's way.
- that it is helpful to the pupil's learning if he gets the opportunity to write, on occasions, for audiences other than the teacher.
- that when he does write for the teacher he need not always be expected to see the teacher as examiner or assessor.
- that these last few points have strong implications for the way we set up and the way we receive pupils' written offerings.
- that setting up situations in which children communicate in a motivated way about what they are learning is difficult. It is one of our major tasks to learn how to do it.

From Talking to Writing

Peter Medway

Introduction

Of all the many reasons why writing goes on in schools, undoubtedly the main one is the belief that people must learn to write when children, because they will need to write when adults. Because this has seemed self-evident, writing has had an easy passage in schools: generally held to be a good thing, it hasn't had to justify its pervasive presence in diverse parts of the curriculum.

But this blanket approval is wearing thin: Midwinter* points out that plenty of adults don't in fact need to write, and individual teachers are coming to say that, whether or not writing is needed in adult life, *their* job is to teach science, history or whatever—not writing; so if writing is to stay in their bit of the curriculum, it will have to earn its keep by producing tangible pay-offs in terms of the learning of science etc., and not only in the learning of writing.

So it becomes necessary to face this question: if we leave aside the justification for writing now as a training for writing later, do we still, on other grounds, want children to write in school? The case now looks weaker.

If instead of 'writing' we said 'language activity', it would be different: support would be readily forthcoming. We now know how language can be crucial to learning and how the knowledge, information and experience which the child meets in school need to be gone over in his own language if they are to be understood. But when we say 'language' in this context, isn't it talking we tend to be thinking of? And isn't it talking rather than writing that presents itself as the obvious language mode for most learning situations?

* E. Midwinter, *Projections*, 1972.

The Case for Talk

The argument for talk as the essential and dominant medium of learning is powerful. One teacher, in discussion with a member of the Project, put it like this:

> Talk is very precious, isn't it. It's the thing that a lot of the kids really come to school for, the chatting round the table. In a way sometimes you really feel you're interfering and interrupting something that's very valuable . . . they're just chatting about the telly or whatever.
>
> Why is this whole Project called 'Writing across the Curriculum'? Why is it not 'Learning across the Curriculum'? . . . We give writing a hugely inflated place. It is *not* as important as children's talking, it is not as important in learning, I don't think, as talking is. It's a very artificial thing . . . If I have an idea or if I think about what I do, I do it either in talking or by thinking. The actual business of writing it down is totally irrelevant. I can see the business that it might well extend me if I did it. But it's not something that there is a pressure for.

It is indeed a great advantage of talk that it generally 'comes naturally'; and it's quite true that although as teachers we may preach the value of writing, our behaviour suggests this belief doesn't go very deep: in *our* dealings with knowledge, information and experience we *don't* habitually resort to writing.

THE CASE OF DAVID

One of us talked to a thirteen-year-old boy, David, in the second year of a comprehensive school, a boy who was unusually conscious of the processes which were contributing to his education. He was an intelligent boy with an impressive range of knowledge and a keen desire to learn. Yet whereas he understood well, and could explain the way talking helped him to learn, he saw no educational value in the process of writing.

Interviewer	But don't you find that when you're writing you put things down in a different way than you could if you're talking?
David	I think that talking brings out more things in you than just writing it down on a piece of paper. I mean you write it down to show the teacher that you've done it but it doesn't bring out any more knowledge in you, I don't think. Well, just getting a piece of paper, saying, oh, I'll write this all down, you know, and just to show the teacher that you've done it and he just ticks it and you've done that bit of work. I think that you, if you just got a book out and read it all through and you told the teacher you'd read the book that should be enough instead of saying, OK David, you've done the book, right, now get a piece of paper and write all about the book, I think that . . .
Interviewer	Yes, I can see that. There's no point in writing down what you know but what about writing down your ideas? You haven't got them in a book but they're about things in the book. Now suppose you . . .
David	I think you could do that, you could do that in taped discussion do that. A taped discussion.
Interviewer	Just to say what you think more easily.
David	Yes, rather than writing it down, because you have to write it in words when you write it down, but say it out. It comes out of you when you're speaking, it just . . . Writing it down takes you half an hour to think what you're doing and in taped discussion you're put on a spot and you can say all about it.

'Talking brings out more things in you': partly because it's less laborious—you can 'get through' a lot more in half an hour's talk than you can in half an hour's writing—and partly because it makes you come out with things you didn't know you knew, or generate completely new thoughts (by contrast with writing, which, he says, 'doesn't bring out any more knowledge in you'). The reason you think when you're talking is, he says, because 'you're put on a spot': that is, your interlocutor makes demands of you, challenges your statements, making you reconsider or clarify them; sometimes he selects the ground you have to operate on, brings in considerations you hadn't previously taken account of and forces you to accommodate them in your thinking. This situation, although demanding for all the reasons mentioned, nevertheless, David feels, produces a relatively *painless* flow of thought: the mental processes seem to look after themselves, and, without much conscious effort, 'you can say all about it'. Writing, on the other hand, is characterised by none of these advantages: mechanical and pedestrian, it gropes along in the dark, with no-one else to help it along in its progression from thought to thought.

So David feels, and we can go along with a lot of it. But mightn't these aids and supports which talk affords sometimes become constraints? Constraints from which *writing* might offer a release?

The Case for Writing

Consider the activity of writing and what it involves, and the points in the education process where it might, by virtue of its distinctive features, be expected to fulfil a need. We can start by thinking of the obverse of David's *pro*-talk points.

'It comes out of you when you're speaking'. Yes—sometimes—but talk has no sooner come than it has gone again. It is evanescent, and this places a severe limit—a limit connected with the duration of short-term memory—on the coherence and organisation one can give to an extended passage of thinking. While the process involved in writing is similar in one basic respect, that language comes up continuously in the mind and the thought is constantly moving on, it is also different in that a record is left of what has passed—footprints in the sand, if you like. As a result, the writer can at any point stop and look back to see where he has come from and get his bearings. He can inspect how the whole construction is getting on, what parts are complete and what remains to be done, what the balance looks like, whether it is consistent, whether it stays on the point, whether anything has been left hanging in the air. On scanning back he can sometimes see connections between things he has said which he was not aware of when he said them, and this may modify what he goes on to say. When he pauses he can put himself in the position of a reader, in order to judge the effectiveness of the communication and give himself some feedback.

But in any case what David says isn't always true. It doesn't always come out of you when you're speaking. It may be *hard* to say something—for a variety of reasons: people differ greatly in their ability to talk in different contexts; the particular social situation may be inhibiting; what one has to say may not have reached a degree of clarity which allows it to be put into words at speed and off the cuff; or may be complicated and involve intricate argument or the deployment of facts and figures.

Writing provides the leisure to search for the best way of saying what you mean. It is of course true that in expressive *talk* a speaker may sometimes generate a variety of alternative ways of saying something and say them one after the other, peppering round the target-meaning with a hail of near-misses; and it may not matter (if your audience is undemanding and sympathetic to your efforts) that everything you say—both what you mean and what you don't mean—'goes out' and can't be taken back. Writing nevertheless *extends* one's power to find the right words. A variety of alternatives may come up in succession in the mind but then a promising one can be written down. It is now in the bag and can't get away, and one can securely continue the search: something better may suggest itself, in which case the first idea can be cancelled; if not, it is there to go back to. What seems the best formulation at the time may not look so good when seen in the light of what one finds oneself saying later: one can go back and change it. What one really wants to say can finally be pulled clear of the debris of rejected words and phrases, and, when 'run through' by the reader (or by the writer as his own reader), will flow like silver-tongued speech, displaying no sign of the mess and sweat of its making.

'You're put on a spot', David says. In other words, the demands made by the person you are talking to make you say clearly what you mean and make you justify your ideas. True: but as we've already suggested, in some stages of one's thinking such demands may be more than one can cope with. Some spots are too hot. One may want to be very exploratory; the thought one is formulating or the line one feels oneself getting on to may be so tenuous or so fragile that at the slightest interruption it will be lost; and the other person's concerns will rarely be quite on all fours with yours; he may sidetrack you, or merely fail to pick up the point you want to follow.

It may be seen as an argument against the use of writing for exploratory or tentative thinking that the written utterance is more 'weighty' than talk, in that what is written is 'on record' in a way that spoken words are not. On the other hand, if you're not going to show your writing to anybody, or only to someone you don't feel anxious about, you can say what you like without fear that you'll be held accountable for it. The absence of an immediate audience can be liberating. You can try out ideas or comments—to see what they feel like, or because you think they are probably right but you want to be sure before you utter them in public. And you can write private things or things which hardly anyone else would be interested in, purely to resolve something for yourself. And you can say things in writing which would, if you spoke them, sound pretentious or inconsistent with your habitual social role (a role which, in the case of a school pupil, may reflect restrictive peer group norms).

Finally, two points about writing which David doesn't touch on.

First, in writing you can take on a fictional role and explore situations from another person's point of view. (You can in drama too, of course—but in rather different ways). Or, without going to the extent of an overtly fictional role, you can try alternative possible stances for yourself. (So you can in normal social intercourse: but beyond certain limits you will be considered to be insincere or to have lost touch with reality). This is another way writing can provide a 'low-risk' situation.

Secondly, it is above all in writing that language can be used for artistic purposes. The spoken language in our culture does allow, to a certain rather limited extent, for the poetic function, particularly in the recreation and shaping of experience in story-telling. But most of the modes of poetic statement available to us depend on writing. In education, language enables the initial uncovering and the tentative examination of new ideas, thoughts and feelings to be carried forward to a definition, or a synthesis, or a provisional conclusion, in two ways: by the attainment of a *theoretical* level in the discursive organisation of thought, or of a *poetic* level in the symbolic or non-discursive mode. The latter certainly is likely to depend on a mastery of the process of writing.

All this amounts to a good *prima facie* case for writing in education. It's a good case, at least, if you accept that schools need to make provision for thinking to go on above ground, which for the most part means in language. Of course, there are those pupils who will do very well by just thinking—they're the ones who have done very well in the past. But what they've been doing inside their heads others manifestly haven't been doing, and it's the latter who we have to take deliberate action to help. Getting them to talk and write is part of the answer to the problem of enabling them to think, since these processes *involve* thinking and yet, unlike the 'pure', chin-on-fist type of thinking, may be got going and kept going in all sorts of ways and with all sorts of different motivations and reasons.

If that's accepted, the next step is to see that there are things that need to happen (sorts of 'thinking'—using that term to mean a wide range of mental processes) that can't be expected to happen in talk. The reasons why they can't, really reduce themselves to two: 'too complex' or 'socially impracticable'. 'Too complex': there are meanings which can't be expressed in talk because you can't hold enough in your head to get a coherent organisation (this holds of both transactional and poetic language). 'Socially impracticable': there are things one can't say because one doesn't say that sort of thing—not necessarily because it's *inconceivable* that one should say it but maybe just because the social contexts one finds oneself in don't lend themselves naturally to it. Telling a fictional story, playing a role, going over something others wouldn't care to hear about, saying things that might get mocked, or ignored—these are situations in which you mightn't feel happy to use talk.

On considering the potential contribution of writing, one is forced to the conclusion that the current disenchantment is due less to the lack of a good case for writing than to the fact that we haven't been very good at it: we haven't succeeded on a big scale in getting kids into writing—certainly not the ones who would most benefit from the use of such overt language processes.

So in the remainder of this paper we turn our attention to that: how do we get children to be able to write? We're not thinking at this point of the problem of the child who can hardly write words at all, serious though that also is, but of the large number of those who are literate but don't write to any effect or with any satisfaction—like David.

Strikingly aware of the strengths of talk, David had failed to discover those of writing. His experience of writing had evidently not given him any glimpse of the enhanced powers he might enjoy with its aid. On the contrary, for him writing represented a *reduction* of his powers. When he turned to writing the gift of tongues was withdrawn: the resources which made him a fluent and effective talker were suddenly rendered unavailable.

There is surely something very surprising about this state of affairs—one which affects many others besides David. After all, the part of the operation which one would suppose to be most difficult, and the almost universal achievement of which is so remarkable, is the capacity to say things *at all*, in whatever form: to come up with language and think in the open with words. Yet this is the part that *everyone* can do (apart from brain-damaged people and other obvious exceptions). By the side of this impressive competence which has already been achieved by all school-age children, the special difficulties of this or that *mode* of language look trifling. With writing one would expect some problems—but one would expect it would be the psychomotor process and the 'coding' that would give the trouble. But this obstacle too David and others like him have already surpassed.

The *extra* problem involved in becoming a motivated writer for someone who *can* talk and *can* write (in the narrower sense) one might expect to be easily surmounted—indeed, the progression might almost be expected to occur of its own accord. One is led to wonder whether what ought to be happening fairly naturally is for some reason being *prevented*. Could it be that, far from failing (despite valiant efforts) to get children to achieve something difficult, we are unwittingly stopping them from doing something easy?

From Talking to Writing

In order for children to make the transition from talking, which they can do, to writing, which we want them to, two conditions will have to be met—or so one would suppose. The 'writing situation' will have to be close enough to a familiar task situation for the same skill, the same knowing how to go about it, to be operable; and yet the writing must produce for the writer some benefit or satisfaction which he couldn't equally have achieved by the less laborious process of talking.

We said before that writing has the advantage over talking in two sorts of situations. In both those situations writing would be felt by the writer to be of distinctive and special usefulness. But one of them—the structuring of complex thought—is perhaps unattainable by any but *experienced* writers: you're doing something which *hasn't got an equivalent* in talk, and you can only even get a sense of the possibility of doing it when you're well inside the special world of the written language.

So it must be the other type of situation we rely on to provide the satisfactions which will enable children to see the point of writing: that is, writing to do things which aren't *theoretically* impossible in talk but which social constraints and habitual ways of behaving work against. And here we must record that in infants and junior schools many children are in fact turned on to writing this way—by writing stories, and things about themselves and what they've done and what they've seen, which are quite like the spoken language in their expressiveness and general feel, but which it would perhaps be unusual to find actually *spoken* by a child. The satisfaction for the writer lies not in the attainment of complexity but in the opportunity to work out what he wants to say and savour it as he goes without having to concern himself with the demands of a *present* audience.

In that sort of situation the child can use all the skill and knowledge he has gained in thousands of spoken transactions. He's doing in writing something which does at least resemble the sort of thing he knows people do in talk. He is still using language to perform a relatively familiar function.

Whose Purposes Does Writing Serve?

But consider how David sees the function of the written language. It's very noticeable how, whilst he sees talk as meeting *his own* needs—helping him to think, showing him how much he knows, increasing his knowledge by 'bringing more out of him'—writing merely meets the *teacher's* needs: specifically, the need to evaluate what has been learnt: a reasonable requirement, no doubt, but one which doesn't get the pupil any further. So writing for him serves a function remote from the normal functions of most (familiar) language: one explicable only in terms of the institutionalised procedures of schools, and one irrelevant to his own learning needs.

Is his problem with writing, then, *not* the psychomotor skill, *not* any difficulty with the vocabulary or structure of the written language, but the unfamiliarity and apparent futility of the use he is called on to put it to?

A look at another case may be helpful at this point.

A SECOND CASE: CHRIS

Chris (aged fifteen, same school) also objects to the normal run of school writing and can't bring himself to do it. For him as for David, writing to show others what you already know you know is an unmotivating assignment. Specifically he objects to the sort of answers required on worksheets. But, unlike David, Chris is a writer: he frequently and by his own choice writes poems and imaginative documentaries. But, interestingly enough, he tends to do so only in sociology, where he isn't really supposed to, and not in English, where he is and where 'stimuli' (such as photographs) are presented to him for that express purpose. 'The thing is with those photos', he says, 'so many people have done them before. So that you feel yours will just get thrown on the pile, and probably some that are better'. What he is usually called on to write in sociology is short answers setting out information acquired. Instead, Chris chooses to invest the information with personal meaning and to create an experience rather than transmit (re-transmit) facts with his words.

Here is an example of what he wrote after looking at a picture of old Leicester in a teacher-produced pamphlet. Notice the adventurous and experimental spirit in his use of language: isn't this to be seen in the light of his strong feeling that it's his *own* piece of work, undertaken for *his* satisfaction?

> *What does a pictorial look of 17th century Leicester show?*
> Who would have recognised the shabby state of what was to become of the ground, that of the popular site of the clock tower.
>
> The ground was cold, the hard-worn pebble stones lay, matching like a jigsaw, brown and old, streets separated, the black-brown finish was the stone face of life. The smell and dirt of a booming industry, spread around settling like rot. The tarnished city welcomed a face lift, this was to happen in due time, still life went on.
>
> The brick-work was choc-a-bloc, crammed to its limits. Windows were square, wooden frames lived between them, tarnished glass, eyes to the centre windows were small as many as 20 smaller panes of glass enclosed at the frames.

The windows being supported by vertical, onend bricks, these outstanding from the rest. The main structure of the building going horizontal. The large baywindows looked out to the front, showing off its area of glass and mass supports, many intricate and finely detailed. The wood finish gave the finishing touch.

The idea of adding a coat of paint to the house was never thought of. Money was small and very little was felt. There were far more important things to buy. Brown, black, grey the colours of the environmental waste and fumes of the not-so-far-away industry.

Letters, words and signposts hung everywhere the direct method of promoting products of the many. Employers names looking outward to the eyecatcher. To live you had to make money and the only way to do this, is to show and let everyone know what and who you are.

Stone slabs round the edge of the buildings. Curbs being flat, straight, the object of the rectangle. The gaps between bricks described the state of living, dark, small, unclean, infinite ending, the manufactured brick described poverty.

Chris talked about his writing with his teacher and a member of the Project team (PM). Here is part of the conversation.

Teacher		Do you like showing it [your writing] to people?
Chris		If it's different from everybody else's, but if it's the same it's pointless. I mean I wouldn't have shown you these if it were just full of answers like everybody else's. It's different.
PM		What do you think about writing down just factual answers? What's your attitude?
Chris		You've not got the feeling there for it. Unless you go into real detail.
Teacher		What do you mean though, you haven't got the feeling?
Chris		Well, the pamphlet's just missed a word and you say do this and write it and you move on to the next page, you've just passed it like that, whereas . . .

PM	It's had no effect on you, no impact.
Chris	Yes. If you write poems and this that and the other, you've got a wider scope and you feel as if you've done something. You've learnt something, you know.
Teacher	You said, if you have just done your task there, and you've gone through it, you wouldn't have got the feeling.
Chris	I wouldn't.
Teacher	What feeling?
Chris	As if you're not part of it, as if you're just a schoolkid and it's doing reams of work. Whereas, if you do it this way, you're doing something creative as well as putting the fact down.
Teacher	So if you're just a schoolkid that's sitting there doing some work, you don't learn, really.
Chris	No. It depends what sort of person you are.
Teacher	But *you* wouldn't.
Chris	I mean I'd sooner write this way. I don't think I could just put one-word answers in. That wouldn't mean anything to me.

What David gets from talking, Chris gets from his sort of poetic writing—namely, the feeling that 'you've learnt something': you've moved on a bit by doing it, you've added something to your understanding. The crucial distinction for him seems to be between, on the one hand, imposed tasks and, on the other, situations where he feels he is saying what he wants to say. For him and for David language flows when they feel they are making a genuine communication—as opposed to a phoney one for someone who doesn't want what you're giving him but merely wants to check up on whether you *can* give it. The normal use of language, after all, the one they've been familiar with outside school, *is* for making real communications; but the implicit complaint of both boys is that school doesn't seem to call for writing to be used for that purpose, the one that it's (in their experience) really for, but is restricted to a special role intelligible only in terms of

A THIRD CASE: NIGEL & GERALD

Several second year classes in a London comprehensive school went out in small groups for a number of mornings to look at the local area. On one occasion, a class made a taped report on returning to school. The situation was relatively formal: the teacher opened the tape with an announcement and called on the boys one by one to report. Despite what could have been a slightly intimidating context, the reports were fluent and lively, combining the expression of interest and often excitement at what had been discovered with precise information about streets, dates, buildings and so on. Reporting developed into discussion, which eventually focussed on a matter which had particularly engaged some of them—the lives of the old people in the area and their feelings about being asked questions by groups of twelve-year-old boys.

But the *writing* that came out of the expeditions was undoubtedly of less interest. It confined itself on the whole to factual report, tended to be short and disconnected, expressed little of the interest and enjoyment that the boys actually felt and failed to set the observations (as the talk had done) in a framework of the meaning and significance the writers attached to them. Somehow the facts they had *talked* about with concern and involvement, in the writing became mere facts, dead information. The expression of excitement isn't necessarily of great value, but it was characteristic of the talk that such expression went hand in hand with a more powerful and purposeful organisation of the information.

Nigel, one of the abler writers in one of the other classes which went out, wrote a number of short accounts about his expeditions with his friend, Gerald. The following piece by him is fairly typical of the sort of thing written by most of the boys—though many didn't have even this subdued sense of involvement (detectable perhaps in the last sentence):

> Greater London Council Ambulance Service was built in 1969. Before it was built for them there was a place called the Red Cross. The red Cross was made into a private service for all over the country. But even before that there was a place called the Cadogan Iron Foundry. There is a peculiar pipe system in the building now, it is a heating system. The pipes come from the RAF runway which they used these pipes for burning lots of paraffin to clear the fog and so the planes can see the runway.

We don't want to say that this is a failure as a piece of writing, merely that it seems meagre and constricted when compared with the talk that was going on—talk which was motivated and expansive, which went into details, made arguments, speculated, looked for reasons, and conveyed the sort of investment the boys had in the inquiry they were undertaking.

Why did the qualities of the talk not carry over into the writing? One of us asked Nigel and Gerald about talking and writing. We had quite a long conversation of which we here give some excerpts.

PM	You were telling me earlier that you go out into Fulham . . .
Nigel	Chelsea.
PM	It's Chelsea, is it, and do investigations and come back. Now when you come back do you have to write about it then?
Nigel	Oh yes, because otherwise it's just like going off of school and just going out, it wouldn't be worth having a school then. So you've really got to come back and do some work. It's a bit boring then.
PM	It's boring?
Nigel	Yes. When you have to write about it.
PM	Yes. Can you give me any idea why it's boring?
Gerald	Well, you already know what it is and sir says write about that, and all you're writing it for really is so when you're doing something else, you

want to look back—you most probably know anyway—you look back in your book and it's got it down there.

This is the sort of mystified view of school work which many children hold: the tasks are right and proper, very necessary and—completely pointless. Notice that Nigel sees the only possible usefulness of the writing as for making a record—a record he'll never use. Like David, he sees the process of writing as one which adds nothing to what he has already.

The interviewer made the point to them that when they came back from an expedition they wouldn't object to *telling* people about it. In fact, they would most likely *want* to tell people—it wouldn't be a burden at all. So why should writing about it be? Wasn't that the same sort of thing?

Nigel   Well, when you tell someone, you don't you sort of put it more in your own words, but when you write about it you've got to think of the same thing that happened.

Nigel seems to be saying that in writing it's necessary to confine yourself strictly to the facts. Gerald seems to pick up this meaning:

Gerald   Yes, if someone tells you something you've got to put their words down. [Presumably he's thinking of reporting on an interview.] If you're telling anything, anyone, you can sort of put a little bit in to make it more exciting if something's happened to you.

Nigel   Say that if you're writing about say a factory, right, and you had these old pipings in it from a certain place, well to the other person you'd tell them that, right, and you could add in all the other bitses about what you did over there, but when you do your story you can only . . . write down . . . you can only say that you saw the piping and what it was used for. [By 'story' he seems to mean simply 'account'.]

Nigel takes it for granted that writing in a situation like this has to be *transactional* writing, which operates a particular criterion of relevance: namely that if it's about 'the subject' it's relevant and if it's about you it's not. Yet the characteristics of this sort of writing are not seen by him as what they really are, a rational means which has been evolved for fulfilling certain specialised ends—i.e. as the answer to such considerations as a reader's need to get systematically arranged information about Chelsea, and nothing but that. Rather, he sees them as a matter of propriety. It is a case of 'this is how it's done'. For some reason it has come about that these boys feel the 'correct' or appropriate form of writing to be the one typically employed in books for making needed information available to readers. But their own situation and needs aren't that at all. Their need at this point is surely not to pass on their data to someone else who needs to know it, but to reflect on it and find significance in it for themselves. That's what they were doing in their talk. They were informing each other as well, of course, but their criterion of relevance was mainly personal: in other words, a speaker selected what to say on the basis of what he found significant, and not according to the imagined needs of some hypothetical ignorant listener, one moreover whose purpose in wanting the information remained obscure.

A bit later, Nigel added:

Nigel	Yes, you can't really have [i.e. in your writing] much more than what you've really seen, you know, and what's to do with Enquiry. [Enquiry: the name of the school subject in which this took place.]
Gerald	If you're telling it to friends, like say Brian in that class, you say, cor blimey we had a smashing time, smashing loads of milk bottles. You can say it to your friends but you can't really write it down, can you?
PM	Supposing you weren't smashing milk bottles, suppose you didn't do anything wrong, but you still said, Cor, we had a smashing time, it was great up there—you wouldn't write that down?

Gerald	Well no, because it just wouldn't seem right, you know, you're writing, 'we climbed over the pipes to look at them and it really was great, you know. It was rather fun, you know'.
	(Omission)
Gerald	You could say, 'we had a very nice time', something like that.
Nigel	Yes, 'very nice time'.

The Power of Unspoken Conventions

But they still haven't really said what makes the difference. Why is it that when they tell someone about it they will convey the whole experience, but when they write it they reduce it to the bare facts, censoring out three quarters of their response? Nigel now tells us what for him is the crucial distinguishing feature of the writing situation.

PM	Why wouldn't you write it down as you would say it?
Nigel	I don't know, it just doesn't sound right, because no-one's going to read it and you just—like a waste of time. You know, it's not worth writing down what nobody's going to read.
PM	But in that case there's no point in writing anything. [i.e. whereas apparently you *do* find some point in writing down the facts.]
Nigel	Well, only what you see, you know, just your work, and that's about it.

When he says 'no-one's going to read it', he doesn't mean that literally: he knows very well that his teacher will certainly read it. The striking thing is that that doesn't seem to count as someone reading it, presumably because the *unspoken convention* of such school writing is that it should purport to be addressed not to the person who is actually going to read it (the teacher) but to a hypothetical public audience (about which nobody has any illusions that it exists); or perhaps not to an audience at all—the writer is just 'writing it down', rather than writing to or for someone. The teacher's position in this transaction between pupil and x, or pupil and no-one, tends to be that of onlooker rather than addressee: he watches how the pupil handles himself in relation to his imaginary public audience, and comments, as it were, from the outside.

Now, a child who is an accomplished writer may in fact be able to write from his school desk in a way which is entirely appropriate for a 'public audience': such writing really could go out into the world and stand on its own and make sense to any interested reader as a genuine communication. What the child who can do this has mastered is not so much certain forms of language as an understanding of the sort of relationship which necessarily obtains between a writer and a set of readers who are not known to him but who do now know something of him. The less mature writer has to proceed without that understanding and is reduced to 'putting on' the voice he hears in such writing. He can only mimic the surface features of the language instead of operating creatively from a real sense of the requirements of an unknown reader. Often all that a child has to go on is a vague awareness of the inexplicit requirements of a teacher who, although he is to be the only actual reader, nevertheless apparently may not be addressed in the writing. (Such writing we would place in the audience category: 'pupil to teacher as examiner'.)

Where such a situation obtains it is seldom the result of the teacher's consciously setting out to make it so. Nor is it a sign that the teacher *as a person* is seen by the child as anything but friendly and sympathetic. Rather it seems that this set of assumptions is just in the 'educational' air: seldom examined, it is unconsciously held by the participants in all writing situations where 'facts' are involved— unless a *deliberate* decision is taken to fight against it. It is unlikely that the teacher of Nigel and Gerald ever explained to them that he wanted them to exclude the expression of personal attitudes in their writing. Indeed, he would almost certainly have held the opposite view that signs of interest and involvement were all to the good. Moreover, he was interested in their writing. He responded to it in a *personal* way and showed them unmistakably that he valued it. He was not seen by the boys as an intimidating figure—on the contrary. They felt they could relax with him, they liked him and they said on the tape that they thought they were lucky to be taught by him. Yet despite all this they never questioned their assumption that their writing for him had to operate under all sorts of constraints which did not affect their talk with him or any other aspect of their relationship. Presumably part of the reason is that in the absence of other models they take their notions of writing from whatever relevant adult writing they meet—in this case, probably, the transactional writing of information books, magazines, newspapers, guidebooks, etc.

It is not surprising that Nigel and Gerald were unable to draw on what they *can* do in language if they see the task as writing for no real purpose and no real audience in a way that results in no advance over the knowledge and understanding they had when they started. But, fortunately, they don't see all writing situations that way. In another context, Nigel feels that his writing performs a real function and provides his reader with something the reader does not already have. And here the adult models he has come across are more helpful: they show him a way of structuring his content that enables him to utilise, instead of forcing him to leave behind, the language of his speech—its rhythms, its expressiveness, its way of putting things. At home with the language he is using, he is not at a loss for what to say. His communication turns out to be effective, and, indeed, capable potentially of speaking to a wide and unknown readership. This poem arose out of the same series of excursions into the surrounding area, and was written for the same teacher. (Spelling corrected.)

Age

Poor old dearie
Down Dunn Road,
She don't have no fun

                                    Nothing I can do,
                                    Says every known being
                                    They don't care a damn

She tries her best
not to moan,
But she has to

           She hates all the old,
           She don't mind the young,
           She likes the young ones.

Some things are hard
Some things aren't
She don't care.

           I don't mind her.
           Does she like me?
           That remains to be seen.

Here she comes
all dressed up,
Snigger! all in rags.

           She's going shopping,
           She can't afford much,
           Enough to keep her alive.

Look how they pass her,
Not saying a word,
In their mind it's, OLD HAG

           How much longer,
           Can she live,
           poor old soul

She's going to tell me
Something now.
What can it be?

           "What yer looking at, eh!"
           "Nothing mam,"
           She's going

THANK GOODNESS

FOR THAT

It Feels Like Him Speaking

    The reason Nigel is able to accomplish this successfully, and in a way that uses the language skill that he has, is likely to be that it represents an extension and modification and extra shaping of the way he habitually speaks, and not an operation on alien territory. When he was a talker it came out and he could say it: he could say what he wanted to say and he found himself *with* something to say—the two come together. Though now a writer, he still feels himself to be in that situation—and this because he has developed sufficiently as a writer to make a verbal construct which he *couldn't* have produced in any talking situation. He has entered the special world of writing and got far enough in to be experiencing 'ways of saying' which have no reflection in the world of talk: nevertheless he has been able to take his familiar equipment with him. His strength is that, although he has here produced a piece of language he would never have uttered in speech, *it still feels to him like him speaking*, not someone else: not some assumed persons or put-on voice forced on him by the need to say these things or cope with this situation. It is relevant that he feels free, because of the climate the teacher has created, to write in the grammar of his own speech, a grammar which, incidentally, is not 'bad English' but the dialect of a speech community comprising several million native Londoners. (Being urban and thriving doesn't stop it being a dialect: dialects don't *have* to be gasping their last breath in the mutterings of an ancient thatcher somewhere out in the sticks.)

Growth from the Expressive

Here then is a school writer working his way into the poetic function by a process of refinement and selection on a strongly established base of *expressive* language. If he continues to develop in this way, his language will retain its life and its purposefulness even though the form will get more specialised. It is likely that the best *transactional* writing also develops this way, gradually advancing from the expressive with lines of communication kept open—rather than taken on fully formed from new models unrelated to one's past language experience.

However, in this paper our concern is not how we may get children to the stage of mature poetic and transactional writing but how we can get them to write at all in any way that enables them to experience the usefulness and satisfaction of writing. The attainment of the differentiated functions of mature writing is another problem: many children don't even get to first base.

A FOURTH CASE: JOHN

John, who was engaged on the same project as Nigel and Gerald, wrote extensively. For whatever reason, he felt able to use writing in the way David said he could use talking. He did not see it as a laborious and artificial process—he enjoyed it. John's relationship with his teacher was an especially good one, and this may have been important in freeing him from anxieties about his writing which he might otherwise have felt. (John said of his teacher, 'I know him and I know what he's like. He's a good man, and he's got the same feelings as me'.) About writing he said:

> ... if I wrote it down, I mean, don't miss anything, just keep thinking, you know what I mean, but when you talk you tend to stutter, you know what I mean, and lose your words and that, you know, things like this.
>
> When I write things down, all the time I think to myself, oh, it's good, you know what I mean? It's great when I write this down.

John feels things strongly and has a lot to say: he talks readily and is an important person in class discussions. His problem seems to be that he has *more* to say than he can easily cope with in talk; and also perhaps that he sometimes wants to say things which the language of his peer group is not accustomed to carrying. The result is that his speech, while forceful and animated, is full of false starts, breaks, fillers to give him a breather while he thinks, and phrases which perhaps disclose an uneasiness about his exposed position in saying unconventional things. Writing apparently provided him with a relief from the aspects of talking that he found uncomfortable.

John spoke in the discussion that was taped and later wrote about what had struck him on his investigations in the area. Here is one of the things he said in the discussion. It illustrates both the sort of things he is prepared to say and the pressure he finds himself under in trying to think at the same time as he communicates:

> The old lady, I mean the old people, they like the young kids to come along and that and have a talk with them because they know that we we we we we care for them, you know what I mean, and we like them, you know what I mean, and this is why they're happy, but when we've gone, like this lady who we met last week, we just, we was having a nice chat, she was happy, you know what I mean, telling about her, well afterwards she was she was all on her own, you know what I mean, lonely, and just, you know what I mean, unwanted, just like that.

To conclude, here is John's writing. It is expressive writing. Facts, observations and information are all there and are effectively communicated but the drive behind this flow of explanation, comment and speculation is a strong *interest* in the topic; and the situation which enables him to talk it out on paper is the availability of a trusted audience. (It appears that he begins by writing 'bare facts' and *becomes* involved as he gets into it.)

It is actually two pieces of writing, done on separate days. Spelling and punctuation have been corrected to make it easier to read.*

> After the war the Germans came over to Britain and built Fulham Gasworks. With it they built a square called the German square. Now it is called Imperial Square. In the Square there are gas lamps and they are still working. They still have gas in them. Some people said that the gasworks

* Readers may wonder what the uncorrected version looked like. Here are the first few lines in the original:

> After the war the Germans came over to britain and built Fulham Gas Works with it they built A square called the German square now it is called imperial square in the square there are Gas laps and they are still working they still have Gas in them. Some people said that the Gas works might be pulled down all along Micheal Rd + Harwood Rd the houses are going to be pulled down

might be pulled down. All along Michael Road and Harwood Road the houses are going to be pulled down because they are going to build a flyover. The old lady in No. 9 Imperial Square said that she doesn't care if they are going to knock down the house because she has had her happy days and now she is old and she is no longer wanted. No-one loves her. Her house has been standing for a hundred years. All the houses in Imperial Square have been standing up for a long time. The people there complain about the supporters come through Imperial Square and they smash bottles and other bad things. This lady said that when the Germans were there it was very hard to get a job. You had to get up very early to queue up to get a job in the power station. It must have been very hard for the people. They might have to wait about six hours before the gates open, then they might not still get a job. I would not like to been in those days. I bet their houses were running with rats. They had no food hardly, their clothes were dirty, they were dirty, they had diseases. It must have been terrible for them. I felt sorry for the lady who we was talking to. It must have been hard for her. People from everywhere came to the Gasworks to get a job. Where my friend lives, his name is Leslie, at the end of his street called Elb Street there is a place there, it has gas there, they put it in the lorries. That has been standing for about a hundred years, and Langford School, that was built in 1889. I used to go there and my brothers went there. I like that school. I will remember that school. Lots of old ladies must have memories but if they tell you they might think that we think the things they are saying to us is silly. It is sad for some of the old people. Their husbands have died in the war and now they have no-one to talk to. They are all alone but this is life. No-one can live for ever. It's very sad. Where I live in Pearscroft Road there is a place called Bulow Court. Before that was built there was a road going through there called Bulow Road. There must be something done about these old people. I don't know what but something.

5 February 1973

I was walking down Townmead Road and I saw a church. It

was called St Michael's Church. It had a little stone on the side of it. It had some words. It said, To the glory of God this stone was laid by Lady IDA DAZZELL, March 23 1899. And in Bronten Road some of the houses are going to be knocked down because the new flyover is going to be built. Quite a lot of houses are going to have to be knocked down. Some old houses are really bad. They have cracked walls, windows smashed and people still live there, but some are good. Some people paint their old houses and they come up very nice. All the houses in Imperial Square are very well done up. They have nice and tidy gardens. It looks really good and it would be a shame to knock these down. I hope these people will put up a fight to keep these houses up. They could get all the people there to demonstrate, make a fight. They really must do something to keep the houses up. The old people do not mind all that much because they're too weak to fight and like I said before they have had their happy days. And along Townmead Road the houses are going to be knocked down again because of the flyover. One of the boys in our class, his is going to be knocked down. His name is Derek Pinder. Some old people like young boys to come up to them and have a chat with them. They think 'Ah, this is nice of them to come up to us and say hello. I don't know why they talk to us, we're just boring old ladies that get on their nerves'. These are the things they think about. Young boys like to talk to old people. They have so much to say about themselves, about when they were little children. I went up to a man. I asked him if he liked London. He said that he loved London. He had lived in London all his life. He was ninety years old. He looked a bit upset, I don't know what about. I asked him if it was hard to get a job when he had left school. He said that when he left school they would do just odd jobs, go around asking if they wanted any help with their shopping or do shopping for them. They could find lots of things to do, but they would not get a lot. When they had got a little bit older it was very hard. Everywhere he went he could not get a job, he said. Life was hard then and lots of things have changed.

Keeping Options Open:
Writing in the Humanities
Pat D'Arcy

Patterns of Writing in Secondary Schools

The Schools Council Writing Research project, based at the London Institute of Education, set out to describe the kinds of writing produced in school, in all subjects of the curriculum, by pupils of 11 to 18 years. Believing that the ability to write was not a single all-embracing ability, as is sometimes assumed, but rather a cluster of related abilities, they tried to find ways of distinguishing the process of writing in one way (of writing a sonnet for example) from the process of writing in another (say a note to the milkman). As they worked out possible categories they applied them to a sample of over 2000 pieces of written work collected from 65 secondary schools scattered throughout the country. In the final stages, when the set of categories was agreed upon, all the pieces of writing were sorted by teachers in accordance with the descriptions supplied to them. The degree of agreement was high enough to satisfy the researchers that the distinctions they had tried to make among the writings were real and could be discerned.

We have described in an earlier pamphlet, *Why Write?* the two sets of categories of writing the Unit devised, the first a division by *function* (what the writing's for) and the second by *sense of audience* (who is it for?). We go on here to report some of the results obtained when the categories were applied to the 2000 pieces of writing that composed the sample. In doing so, however, we should point out that the restrictions attaching to the sample are such that the figures can do no more than *suggest* the kind of results you might expect to find if you examined the work on another sample of schools. They tell us a good deal about this particular set of schools, and give us a rough idea of what we might expect to find more generally.

It is hardly surprising that the kinds of writing produced in one curriculum subject differ from those produced in another. For the subjects that figured most prominently in the sample, here are the percentages to be found in the three main function categories, taking one subject at a time.

FUNCTION BY SUBJECT—TABLE A

	TRANSACTIONAL	EXPRESSIVE	POETIC	MISCELLANEOUS
ENGLISH	34	11	39	16
HISTORY	88	0	2	10
GEOGRAPHY	88	0	0	12
R. I.	57	11	12	20
SCIENCE	92	0	0	8

It was one of the chief intentions of the Writing Research Project to provide a description of writing which could be used in plotting the way children develop in their ability to write. The following table is again concerned with the main function categories, but shows how the percentages change (taking alternate years) from the beginning to the end of secondary schooling (in these particular schools).

FUNCTION BY YEAR—TABLE B

	TRANSACTIONAL	EXPRESSIVE	POETIC	MISCELLANEOUS
YEAR 1	54	6	17	23
YEAR 3	57	6	23	14
YEAR 5	62	5	24	9
YEAR 7	84	4	7	5

From these two tables it is clear that in some subjects the tasks set by these teachers were almost all transactional ones, and that in all subjects taken together the number of transactional tasks increased considerably throughout the years at school. This category, in fact, dominates the work. We find a similar pattern for one of the sense of audience categories, that of the teacher as examiner: the two features are likely, we suggest, to be two ways of revealing a single tendency. Here are the percentages for sense of audience categories taken a year at a time.

AUDIENCE BY YEAR—TABLE C

	Trusted Adult	Pupil-Teacher Dialogue	Teacher as Examiner	Peer Group	Public	Miscellaneous
YEAR 1	2	51	40	0	0	7
YEAR 3	3	45	45	0	1	6
YEAR 5	2	36	52	0	5	5
YEAR 7	1	19	61	0	6	13

We might tentatively conclude that there is also a connection between the small and generally declining percentages in the teacher as trusted adult category in this table and the similar figures for writing in the expressive function in table B.

If we compare our hopeful expectations with the findings in general, it seems that two major comments must be made. First it is disappointing to find that in a set of what was in fact ten categories of sense of audience two of those categories alone (and both of them 'teacher' categories) absorbed 92% of the writings.

Secondly, we cherished particular views about the educational value of expressive writing. Whether in talk or writing expressive language is *par excellence* the language of discovery, of exploring and trying out new ideas; and when it comes to writing, it seemed to us that the expressive, being the form of writing nearest speech, had a key role to play as the matrix from which more sophisticated forms would be, by a process of increasing differentiation, developed as more experience was gained. This hypothesis on the part of the research team could certainly not be corroborated from the evidence: expressive writing in the first first year amounted to no more than 6% of the work—and that leaves little scope for the fanning out they had looked for.

What sort of tasks are the pupils performing when they write transactionally? The sub-categories of this function give us some idea of the range of possibilities.

```
                    TRANSACTIONAL
        ┌──────────────┴──────────────┐
     INFORMATIONAL                 CONATIVE
1. RECORD                        (PERSUASIVE)
2. REPORT                        1. REGULATIVE
3. GENERALISED NARRATIVE OR DESCRIPTION   2. PERSUASIVE
4. LOW LEVEL GENERALISATION
5. GENERALISATION–CLASSIFICATION
6. SPECULATION
7. THEORISING
```

Up to the end of the fifth year almost all the transactional writing in the sample fell into the first five informational categories. It appeared largely to be the pupils' attempts to set down in writing *what they already knew* (and mostly for a teacher audience they knew knew it better). There was rarely any sense that they were engaging in an ongoing dialogue in which new ideas could be aired and explored. Rather the writing was clearly regarded in most instances as an end product— an account of something that had already happened, whether this was an experiment in science or a class discussion or earlier reading—or a day out.

There were hardly any writings by pupils younger than sixteen which could be categorised as speculative, theoretical or persuasive. Does this mean that below that age pupils are incapable of speculation or of putting forward their own opinions on paper? In their concluding remarks on Stage One of the research, the team reflected that 'for whatever reason, curricular aims did not include the fostering of writing that reflects independent thinking; rather attention was directed towards classificatory writing which reflects information in the form in which both teacher and textbook traditionally present it'.

Changing the Audience and the Situation

One of the jobs of the Development Project has been to keep

an eye open for any writing in schools which has played a more
integral part in the individual's efforts to learn than the bulk of
the earlier sample appeared to do. Such writing may fall into any
one of the three main function categories, including the transactional, but it will be more likely to have an audience other than
teacher as examiner and the writer's own thoughts and attitudes
will be there as well, meshed in with the observations and the
facts that he has been confronted with in one form or another—
on a worksheet, perhaps, or in a book or in some way from the
teacher.

On occasions we have suggested to teachers ways in which
the writing audience and situation may be changed from the
'teacher as examiner evaluating information' so that the
nature of the writing task—and of the writing—may change too.
Francis Cleary's report of what happened when woodwork
classes were organised on a shop floor basis for the day is
one such example, and Ricky's spilled out thoughts about his
plans for making his Gnat Killer dagger is another. (See Why
Write?)

In this pamphlet we have collected together some writings
from one of the schools with which we have had close contact—
Countesthorpe College in Leicestershire. As many readers will
already know, the teachers at Countesthorpe had already made
far-reaching audience and situation changes which affected the
ethos of the whole school quite independently of the Writing
Project. As a staff they had agreed from the start that their
relationship with students should be based on a principle of
mutuality and that wherever possible, choice should be built
into the curriculum.

We have obtained, from a small group of pupils studying
Humanities in their fourth and fifth year, writings and comments which we found encouraging for several reasons: they
reflect a wider range of writing audience and function than
generally appears to be the case in the later stages of secondary
schooling; the fact that external examinations were approaching
does not seem to have operated restrictively. We know, in fact,
that the teachers had made a determined effort to keep writing
options open instead of cutting them down. Their success is

reflected in the further fact that we didn't have to hunt for examples; writing of the kind that we quote here was not exceptional. Another heartening indication that writing was regarded fairly widely as an activity that had point and purpose, was that many of the students to whom we talked were enthusiastic about what they had written. They saw writing as a genuine form of communication.

Self Chosen Projects

Significantly perhaps, a considerable part of the students' time in Humanities (basically Social Studies/English) is occupied with project work of their own choosing. They are free to spend as long as they want on a project—collecting materials, discussing their work with the teacher, writing about it. In Susan's case, with her work on old age, the time spent on it in the fourth year varied from week to week—other projects intervened, but in the background there was continuing interest in this particular study, kept alive partly as a result of regular visits to an old people's home and to a 'Tuesday' club at school for local old age pensioners. When I first saw her folder of writing about old age, towards the end of her second term in the fourth year, it contained several accounts of visits she had made, books and articles that she had read and interviews with voluntary groups concerned about old people. She was very clear in her own mind about which pieces she regarded as most valuable and satisfying; those in which she recorded her own visits and encounters with the old. Here is one of her accounts, written soon after she started on this study.

> 10.10.73
>
> B... geriatric hospital is pretty much the same as any other hospital. As soon as I walked in I could smell the cleanliness which literally made me feel ill and depressed.
>
> I would really hate to be put in a place like that, don't get me wrong, the staff are pleasant enough so is the building but the atmosphere is dead! The only entertainment they get is T.V. and each other. None of the patients talk to each other much. Most of the people I talked to said the food was good, the staff were fine but they wanted to go home.

> It is enough to kill anyone being put in a place like that! It is really dull and quiet, nothing seems to happen. The old folks spend all day every day, sitting and looking at one another. Some are out of their minds. One woman lay in bed screaming, she sounded exactly like a monkey in a zoo. It was enough to give me the creeps anyway. Most people had relatives who visited them regularly. If I was the daughter of one of the women there I would certainly hate leaving my mother in a depressed place for even a day. I know that it is difficult to cope with old people and lift them around when you have got families of your own to deal with but I'd rather my parents died at home together or at least in familiar personal surroundings not a place where I would feel I was sent to die anyway.
>
> I would feel that instead of waiting I would want to finish my life quick, die young. Anything to avoid being put in any sort of care.
>
> I walked around like a cheshire cat, a grin or smile permanently fixed on my face, most people must have thought I was mad. I just laughed about any stupid thing. It seems ridiculous to me now, but that is how I felt. I could not help it. I have always had a secret dread for hospitals and would not be too keen on going back to B . . . again!

When I asked Susan whether she felt she'd learnt anything as a result of doing this project she said one of the things that struck her was the way old people seemed to be treated like children 'once they get past the age of sixty—like at the Tuesday club, sort of "come on dear" . . . ' She added that her own attitude to old people had changed too: 'I was more likely to mock them and just laugh at them before, but now I sort of respect them more and feel sorry for them—it's awful'.

There is the strong impression that her contact with old people—both in the hospital, the Home and the club, has given her something to communicate which she has felt and thought about a great deal. When I asked her why she preferred basing what she wrote on her own first hand experience, she said 'because if you get it out of books, then the people marking it . . . know anyway'; about this particular project she commented 'I don't think there's anything in the project that she (the teacher) really knew about. I mean she knows about old age and that, but it's mainly my opinions of old age and what I've found out from old age . . . '

Perhaps it is this sense of freedom to put forward her own opinions, along with the confidence that they will be valued by the teacher, that makes it possible for Susan to 'write as she thinks', her thoughts scanning back over the experience of the visit to discover in retrospect what she has made of it all:

> As soon as I walked in I could smell the cleanliness which . . . made me feel ill and depressed.
>
> I would really hate to be put in a place like that . . . the atmosphere is dead.
>
> It is enough to kill anyone being put in a place like that.
>
> If I was the daughter of one of the women there I would certainly hate leaving my mother in a depressive place for even a day.
>
> I would feel that instead of waiting I would want to finish my life quick, die young.
>
> It was such a release to get out I could not stop myself laughing.

We can see how the recollection of what happened is combined here with self-awareness about her own responses, generalisations which place the hospital in a wider context and speculations about 'what would happen if . . .'

Writing from First Hand Experience

It may be that the need to write in this flexible way (moving from specific details *about* what happened to a variety of comments—analytic, emotive, speculative—*related to* what happened) is more powerfully present when the writing is about the writer's own experience than when it is about someone else's writing, for which, in a sense, the thinking and shaping have already been done. The feeling that there is nothing more to say about what someone else has already said may be why Susan dismissed 'getting it out of books' as 'just boring—just textbook rubbish', although she had in fact written some quite competent pieces based on what she had read. In the piece we have just quoted, however, Susan's own feeling and thoughts had already been directly involved *at the time of the visit*—she is not having to struggle to internalise those of another writer. Further, the school situation encouraged her to value her own responses so that there were no pressures on her to censor them out when she came to write about her visit; hence the expressive* nature of her writing.

Susan's attitude to books is similar to that of a second-year girl who had written an interesting 'bird project' based on visits to various places in the locality. When asked why she had decided to do it, she said straight away 'I knew we'd be going out' and added later that she preferred this kind of project to what she called 'school' projects because 'school projects are boring— there's nothing like going out and things like that—you have leaflets and . . . I get fed up of doing what I know'. Perhaps more children than we realise get the impression that they 'already know' something in the sense that there is nothing fresh to learn, because it is already there—in the book in front of them—all completed and finished before they've even begun on it.

At any rate writing about other writing certainly produces a great deal of generalised classificatory work in school, sometimes perhaps at the expense of more expressive or reflective thinking-it-out-as-you-go writing. By comparison, writing about first hand experience seems to allow for a wider range of audience and function more successfully. We do not want to imply by this that experiences and insights which can be gained at second hand through reading what someone else has written are never of value. All the students whose writings we quote in this pamphlet had read fairly extensively 'round' the subjects which they had chosen. The point we would like to make is rather about the value of reading which *feeds into the ongoing concerns of the reader*; if his interest is aroused sufficiently for him to choose to find other writing about a topic which concerns him, then the gap between writer and reader is already half way to being bridged. It does seem though that extending the field of

---

*Often the threat of 'having to write it up' may not only censor out expressive writing but may also inhibit the thinking that leads to such writing, with the result that any kind of personal analysis in retrospect (about either first or second hand experience) may be discouraged by the expectation that the teacher is only interested in 'the facts'. c.f. Nigel and Gerald, *From Talking to Writing* pp 14–18.

study to include real people and real places ('I knew we'd be going out') has considerable potential for keeping learning options open. It also enables students to find their own ways of assimilating new experiences and thus to convert them into additional 'knowledge'. For this reason we include two further examples (taken from fifth year Community Studies folders) of writing which followed doing rather than reading.

What it's like to be mentally handicapped   Jenny W

I suppose, thinking about it, I've always wanted to know more about mental illness and the handicapped. Also a hidden ambition was I wanted to teach the mentally handicapped. So I thought this a perfect way to get to know in therory about the subject and get to do some practical as well. Ever since a child I've wondered about my uncle who is severely mentally handicapped; and I've seen him in tantrums and moods, so I've grown up with some knowledge; I know a lot of people get awfully frightened at the thought of mentally handicapped people and being with them. Only because society does not accept anything we regard as abnormal and conditions us to reject, put them in a hospital away from the public. Thank goodness, today this is being overcome. I started really doing voluntary work at garden parties for the mentally and physically handicapped, then as my interest in the subject developed I started visiting G . . . hopital from school and now go to the C.A.R.E. village at S . . . just outside Leicester.on Saturdays; And I thoroughly enjoy my work and I am learning more with every visit . . .

She continues in another paper in her folder:

I remember well my first visit to G . . . hospital. It was a dull afternoon in September, cold but crisp. C . . . , a teacher, took us to the hospital. We were laughing and joking all the journey, perhaps because we wished to hide how nervous we were deep inside. The main building is a big house. A long driveway down to the house is surrounded by trees. It looked like something out of a film set. You wouldn't know the occupants were hundreds of mentally ill people.

Eventually arriving, we walked round the grounds with C . . . meeting and chatting to various patients that were walking or keeping themselves busy. We visited the children's ward. A little boy sat outside on the slabs and watched us attentively, not responding to our smiles. I remember the terrible smell in the children's ward. They were in rooms and rushed to the glass door as we approached and pressed their faces against it. Some just sat there in corners and others didn't even notice us.

> We walked past the main house towards the industrial ward where I was to spend my alternate Wednesday afternoons from today. From the outside it resembled a small factory with muffled glass windows and the double main door. Entering I was confronted by the same smell as the children's ward, only not so strong. I felt sure to spend an afternoon in this stench would make me sick. I wasn't sure what to expect. I'd met mentally retarded people before but never worked with them.
>
> We were introduced to Mr A . . . who, with two nurses and a Mr J . . . , ran the occupational therapy. He told us about the occupational ward and its functions. He showed us adjoining rooms where specialist workers made wicker baskets and toys. My first impression of the ward was that it was so drab, very clinical. They had made a bit of an attempt to liven it up with posters and now they've even acquired a radio with speakers but the walls were still that drab grey-green colour. They seemed to be relatively happy and were very anxious to meet us. We made notes and walked around attempting to talk; most of them were very pleased to talk to us. I noticed their need for touch and affection. One girl, D . . . , started to pour out her problems. Now I realise it is her way of acquiring sympathy and attention. To every new visitor she puts on the crying act. They were all partaking in some small activity, e.g. packing cocktail sticks and making boxes.
>
> At about 3.15 they all had tea and one of the women washed up. I found them beautiful people and so affectionate. I soon learnt all their names pretty well and all their particulars, what they did last night, who their boyfriends/girlfriends were. Once you gained their confidence it was all go. You couldn't shut them up, it was great.

Here, as in Susan's writing about her visit to the geriatric hospital, there is varied thinking going on—informative, reflective, perceptive, appreciative.

Jenny B's Visits to Edith

Another girl chose to make a study of the grandmother of one of her friends as her major project for the Community Studies course. Edith was senile and had been taken in by her daughter (Cynthia) as she was quite incapable of looking after herself anymore. Jenny visited Edith regularly (they lived on the same council estate) from September 1973 to February 1974 when the old lady was taken ill and died in hospital. She wrote down what Edith said verbatim, so her diary of these visits, extracts from which are given below, is another kind of first hand writing which makes interesting reading for a more public audience than just the teacher.

18. 9. 73 Persons present: Edith, Cynthia, Penny, Shirley and me

Edith is sitting on the sofa next to Shirley and we're talking about a tall dark handsome bloke we met at Bailey's last night and saying what a Casanova he was and she's saying: 'Yes, he looks that way, he looks like him'. Shirley's just asked her to tell me her life story but she says she don't know how to do it.

She's now rumbleing on . . . 'Oh dear. Arn't you very well, oh, I'm glad you're well'. She's now screwing her face up and looking at her hands. 'One, two, three, four.'

She's now looking at me. 'It's nice, I like it. No, it's all right dear, thank you very much, bless you. Yes. Yes. My word isn't he quick.' She's scratching at her skirt again and Shirley's just told her to stop it so she says 'I see, well they're big you see'. She's just pulled her jumper up to make it look like she's got a big chest, she says 'I like to make a laugh' it's nice cos we're all laughing at her.

She's scratching again and she says 'I've only had one, I don't know where it came from'.

She's just sitting and smiling now, hang on, she's laughing now because Shirley told her that she looks like something out of Psycho.

Shirley's just pulled her nose so she said 'ow, I've only got one nose. I'll have to buy lots of them, thank you very much, gentlemen'.

Everyone's getting fed up of her now so they've told her to shut up. It won't last long though.

1st November

She's walking around the room fiddling about with everything. I'll just ask her what she's doing. 'I've got some to send tomorrow for Americans. Yours was a good, wasn't it Cynthia?' She's just said to Marie 'Can I turn this telly back so it will be another time?' Marie said 'Yes if you want'. 'Oh thank you very much, I'll go and fetch one.'

I'm just going to show her a photograph of herself. She's showing it to me and saying 'It's me, you wouldn't believe it, that's a good one,

I don't look fat there'. She's blowing her cheeks out. 'There I am again, you get sick to death of them, thank you very much dear, thank you.'

25th December

The first thing I'll say to Edith is 'Merry Christmas'. She's just smiling at me. I'll tell her I've got a Christmas present for her and give it to her. 'Thank you dear, mm, yes, mm.' She's put it on her knee. With a bit of help she finally opens it and says 'Thank you. oh it's a nice one isn't it, yes, yes it is' and she put it on her knee again. It's a pity she doesn't understand Christmas, I don't think she really realises her son is here even. Poor thing, still at least she's not spending it alone like many old people will.

26th January

I went round and got the shock of my life, Edith is in hospital. Cynth called the doctor this morning and he sent for an ambulance to take her in hospital because she's got a fractured hip.

29th January

The operation has been cancelled because Edith isn't strong enough. She's got a drip in her, but she looks a lot better, she's more talkative. I'll ask her if she's alright. 'Yes thank you. I'm a lot better, I'm fine. Are you dear?' I'm okay, it's her I'm worried about. She looks very tired I'll ask her if she is. 'Yes, just a little dear.' She's chattering away to herself and I'm very glad for a change. I can't quite make out everything she's saying because she's still not got her bottom teeth in. She's trying to ger her hand out of the covers and she's touching my face now and saying how lovely I am. That's really nice. She's took hold of my hand and I feel really upset, my eyes keep watering. I'll have to say goodbye now. 'Yes dear, goodbye and thank you dear, yes, thank you.'

17th February

Today Edith passed away as far as I know in her sleep. I was very upset when I heard and I couldn't stop crying and thinking about her, even though it probably was for the best.

21st February

Today was Edith's funeral. Edith's two sons, Cynth, Penny and I went went in the funeral car and although it was quiet and sad, it was a

> beautiful funeral with lots of gorgeous flowers. I couldn't believe she was in the coffin.

Why write? It's sometimes difficult to give a good reason when talking or doing or reading would have achieved what is to be learnt just as well, perhaps better. But here, unless Jenny had written down exactly what Edith said and did, she would never have been able to convey so poignantly the old lady's personality—and her plight. Her recorded visits are conveyed sympathetically rather than sentimentally and again the function of the writing is many-faceted. It is partly to inform and in the sense that it records what happens we could classify it as transactional writing. But in so far as the writing is also a vehicle for Jenny's own responses ('I'd love to know what she's thinking about . . . I feel really upset, my eyes keep watering . . . It's a pity she doesn't understand Christmas, I don't think she really realises that her son is here even') the writing is expressive—moving overall perhaps towards the poetic as Edith emerges Ophelia-like from the words on the page.

Interviewing People

Edith was really too senile to be 'interviewed' by Jenny as her mind wandered too unpredictably from one passing thought to another. Our next two pieces are both based on situations in which people outside the school were asked for their views. For Steve (4th year) it was the first time that he had based any project work on his own observations. He comments on his work about 'The Students' Demo' as follows:

> A piece of work like this made a pleasant change for me as it was the first time I have ever done anything from first hand information. I was actually at the Demo and interviewed people instead of reading about it afterwards. I would like to do more of my work in this way . . . I find work of this kind by far the most interesting that I have ever done and feel that it is of more value for these reasons: It helps me with talking to people if I interview them for school work and I will always have to talk to people other than those who I know. If I can go to a protest and then write about it then I can go from there and decide what else I want to know about it. It is like having a

> video-tape of the protest—I have all I want to know (hopefully) on paper and ready for use whenever I want it.

This capacity of written language to capture impressions, and in that sense to hold the options open for further reference and possible modifications later on, was also mentioned by Susan:

> I think it helps to write things down because you can look back and you can remember better from that because if you don't write it down you forget your first impressions of places ... When you go somewhere the first time it's nice after a few times to look back and find—compare your first impressions with the one you've got at the moment ... Then you can do another piece of work comparing the two.

Interviewing people to discover what their opinions are about a particular subject is a kind of half way stage between relying entirely on one's own experience and using books. For Steve it provided him with a number of different angles on the Students' Demo.

> In our interviewing we got three main opinions these are ...
> 1) It's a complete waste of my time and yours.
>   (This came from the two elderly women)
> 2) It's worth trying but I don't think you will get anywhere.
>   (This came from one of the students)
> 3) Yes it is worth it and I think they will succeed.
>   (This came from one of the students and the policeman)

For Alison, who chose to do her Community Studies project on adoption, interviewing two friends of the family who had themselves adopted two children gave her a more immediate contact with the adoptive situation (from the parents' point of view) than simply reading about it could have done, and her sense that she is drawing on real experience is reflected in the writing.

> —After being accepted they had a wait of fourteen months before anything further happened. They had asked for a little boy but Jean said that if she was adopting now she wouldn't make that stipulation. For the first six months after being accepted Jean said that she was really keyed up and ready to receive the baby, but as time went by this faded a little, as Martin said, 'You can't stay pregnant forever!' so when the letter came saying that there was a six week old baby

waiting to be adopted it was a mad rush to get everything ready.

—Martin and Jean had a great deal of support from their close relatives who were all delighted that they were going to adopt and some of their closest friends were already adoptive parents.

—'The only odd comments we got were from people who were near strangers. I remember one distant relative of Martin's before we actually adopted David, but after we had started telling people. He came up to us and said "I think that's a wonderful thing you are going to do! It's very Christian of you" as if we were going to take a poor ragged orphan into our home, when all the time we were desperate to have a child.'

—We talked a bit about matching and Martin and Jean thought that on the whole it was better if the two sets of parents' intelligence was matched so that intelligent adoptive parents with more to offer an intelligent child would have at least as much chance of having a bright child as if he was born to them.

—Finally Jean told me about the most difficult stage of the adoption, 'it was when we were childless. The attitudes we met then were far more hurtful than any we've met since we adopted. It's absolutely amazing how people assume that you are childless by choice. We may have had some tactful friends who never mentioned it but the number of people who said quite openly "Well when are you going to have a family then?" or "It's all very well for you having holidays abroad, you won't be able to do than when you've got a family" things like that at that stage when we were desperately wanting children were very hurtful and at that stage you don't particularly want to say to people that you are trying to have a family and can't, it's very private.'

Anecdote, discussion, honest comments from someone who knows from experience what it's like—it gives a sense of focus to Alison's writing which a more generalised commentary often lacks. She ends her account of the interview with the footnote 'Martin and Jean were extremely interesting to talk to and I learned a great deal from them'. Clearly the chance to discuss what it's like to adopt children had been a valuable experience. Did the writing add anything? It is difficult to be categorical about this—but if Susan's remarks and Steve's are anything to go by ('It's like having a video-tape . . . ', '. . . because if you don't write it down you forget your first impressions . . .'), the act of writing it down may have helped to fix what was said in Alison's mind thus helping her also to be more clearly aware of her attitudes to it. Writing gives a shape which doesn't blur at the edges with the passing of time.

A Range of Writing Opportunities

The writings that have been quoted so far have tended to be in the expressive function because we wanted to show how the flexibility of such a close-to-thought, close-to-talk writing can be be as appropriate and helpful to older pupils as it can to seven or eight year olds. Adolescents like comfortable clothes for playing and working in too—and expressive writing is not dissimilar to this kind of gear in the ease of movement it allows.

The original Writing Research Team have suggested that expressive writing is the matrix out of which the various forms of transactional and poetic writing grow: transactional on the one hand as a tool for *participating* in one way or another in the world's affairs, poetic on the other hand as a means of *contemplating* past experiences and of sharing our memories and reflections with a wider audience.

Susan's writing about her first visit to a geriatric hospital is a real mixture of these two stances—at one moment she is recollecting what happened and standing back to contemplate her feelings retrospectively, at other points in the writing she is speculating about what might happen in the future—almost planning in advance: 'I know that it is difficult to cope with old people and lift them around when you have got families of your own to deal with but I'd rather my parents died at home together or at least in familiar personal surroundings . . .'

This movement between spectator and participant roles is characteristic of writing which is 'expressive', but in some of the other pieces that we have quoted we can see how the *trend* of the writing is moving away from the expressive either towards a more informational or decision-making function or towards a more contemplative one. Steve's writing avout the Students' Demo would illustrate the former and Jenny B's writing about Edith, the latter.

There were examples in the writing of all the students whose work we have used, of pieces that could be classified as dominantly transactional or dominantly poetic. In other words, they were all capable of spreading out across the whole range of writing functions in work of their own choice. Again, the study of a project appeared to encourage this kind of diversity in so far as different writing functions helped the writer to explore the topic from different angles. Steve, for instance, who disliked what he called 'creative writing' (about 'Water and Wind' . . .) had this to say about the relevance of imaginative writing to project work:

> I write stories occasionally—yeh, it does appeal to me writing stories and writing creative things does—if—so long as I can pick what I want to do—you know—if I feel like writing a story . . . it tends to be to illustrate what, er, my factual work's in—say if I did, er, Vietman—a story might be about some Vietnamese child or other whose parents had been killed in warfare or something like that . . . I think it can be as helpful as having the factual thing. You know, one needs the other sort of thing, because I can write as much as I like about this factual thing in Vietnam—what the Americans are using, and what it does to your skin if it's napalm or—and the dates and things, but it still doesn't really explain what life's like in Vietnam—it just gives people a load of facts, a bit like having a computer.

In his own words Steve is explaining how writing in the poetic function is concerned to explore feelings. What he doesn't mention, however, is the other central characteristic of this function —its *presentation* of such feelings in an increasingly formalised fashion as a construct—a work of art which can be offered to the reader partly for him to contemplate and partly for pleasure. Here is an example, a poem written by Jenny B in a context very different from her visits to Edith:

Our love tree

We'd meet at our love tree everyday
And we'd hold hands and talk,
And sometimes, if we were in the mood
We'd go for a little walk.
Those were happy days I remember
In the beautiful days of summer
From June to September.
You bought a penknife one day

And inscribed our names on the tree,
I inscribed I loved you
And you inscribed you loved me.
We were so happy together
With the birds singing
And the lovely weather.
But with less holding hands and talking
We knew it wouldn't last,
So we kissed our love tree goodbye
And left it in the past.
Memories flow back
When I walk by our love tree
As it turns black.

By contrast, as an example of writing which is clearly transactional, here is a further piece from Alison's study on 'Adoptability' to show how, sometimes, generalised classificatory writing can serve an entirely appropriate writing function, especially when the student is basing what he or she writes on material already in print.

Adoptability

Perhaps the most difficult decision to be made directly concerning the child in adoption is whether or not he should be placed for adoption. It is generally agreed that for most children an adoptive home is better then a foster child's home, but it is not always as cut and dried as that. When possible the natural parents are encouraged to keep their child but the fact that the child has been taken into care in the first place indicates some sort of neglect or incapacity on the part of the parents and how does one decide at what point the neglect and rejection of the parents becomes such that it is no longer possible for the child to return home?

There are cases of children who have spent years in care and whose parents rarely or never visit but who still maintain that one day they are going to take the child back. How can it be decided whether or not there really is a parental tie between the child and his parents?

These are just two of the immensely difficult questions that the adoption worker has to answer when deciding whether or not a child should be placed for adoption. There are basically three reasons why many deprived children are not considered adoptible:

a) it is thought that the natural parents should retain their responsibilities

b) on the grounds of the child's health, heriditary background or emotional problems it is felt that adoption is too great a risk

c) the agency does not think that a suitable home can be found.

The subject of parental rights and responsibilities is one that a lot of people feel strongly about. Parents should be held responsible for their children's welfare is the general opinion and probably the right one . . .

This is highly competent transactional writing. Alison's own voice has receded into the background—the language is cool, the tone neutral. Because it is both competent and informative the audience for whom the writing is fully meaningful is public rather than personal—there is no need to rely on any inside knowledge of either the writer or the situation in which she is writing for it to be fully understood. To be able to write impersonally and analytically is certainly one of the increasing number of choices that the developing writer should be able to make.

The Development of Writing Abilities— Steve's Project

Finally to come back to Steve, in order to trace how an individual can develop and become aware of his own capacities to handle written language. He was half way through his fourth year at secondary school when I met him. At that stage he had a fat black ring file full of typewritten work which he had produced mostly since the previous summer. I borrowed this and was impressed by the variety of writings that it contained: reporting, generalising, speculating, putting forward his own opinions and commenting on other writers.

He agreed to jot down brief comments about why he had written each piece and what he had gained from it. In addition, I spent an evening talking to him about his work. The following points emerged.

He placed considerable importance on being able to discuss what he was working on with his teachers; at three different places on the transcript he mentions this point.

> I sit in the classroom and, you know, just talk or discuss things with John* or any teacher who happens to be around. I like discussing things, I find it very useful, I talk to anybody . . .
>
> I find talking to teachers about, well, probably the second most valuable thing, and the most interesting I think.

(And the first most valuable thing would be—)

> Books—but I think that I find talking to teachers or talking to anybody about the—er, most interesting.

In fact Steve does most of his actual writing at home. He uses time in school for collecting materials or for talking.

> I think maybe I've got out of this habit of just getting one book and one worksheet and assuming that's everything—now I've got more into the habit of wandering round the whole school—you pick up interesting things in the science area occasionally, you know—I go to the Resources, I go all round the Pod† —sometimes it's the other Pod —or to the Resources or the Library—I just get as much as I can get and, er, sort it out from there.

He started writing extensively in his third year in the school, but looking back to his first big project (on 'The British Political System') he realises how much he has progressed since then.

> This was the first big project I did and now when I look at it I marvel at how pathetic it was. I say big project because it was bigger than anything I had done before but now when I look at it I realise that to get anywhere near the amount of information that should be in it, actually in it, then it should be a lot longer. I have placed emphasis on the wrong things and made all the mistakes I was warned about . . . But I have learnt more from that project than any other piece of work I have ever done at school so it was only a failure in terms of what it was, not what was learnt from it.

Steve has now discovered how to improve his writing in various ways. He has realised on his own account that he needs to structure it. Since 'The British Political System' he has developed his own methods for organising information gained from books,

---

*his form teacher   †a block of classrooms

which both improve the writing (at the level of structured generalisation) and, more importantly still, help him to assimilate it mentally.

> Well, I have to make a pattern—say this Vietnam project I did, I did a great section on Ho Chi Minh and there was so much information—there were books on it and newspaper articles and he was mentioned in every book about Vietnam and the Vietnam war and everything, so I sort of had to have a pattern in my mind—so what I did was get a bit of paper and wrote down basically what I was going to do about him, just set it out in stages . . . so I've got these bits of paper about all sorts of things dotted about in my folder . . .

Here is an extract from what Steve wrote as part of a longish piece in that project, about 'American Involvement in Vietnam'.

> For a time after the Geneva conference there was a shaky peace in the South and American troops were there called 'Advisors'—they were in Vietnam long after people stopped believing in this term. The Americans had now got themselves into a position that was very hard to get out of.
>
> American aid was first given to the French in Vietnam because the Americans thought they would get rid of the communist elements in the country by doing this, so the biggest nation in the world, a nation that one would expect to set an example was helping a country in the crime of trying to take over another country and even worse they were not helping them because they believed that the country was right in taking over the other country but because they thought that Communism was spreading too fast and they did not want it to spread any more. The situation was really nothing to do with the Americans it was just an excuse to get rid of the communists.
>
> It was stated in the Geneva agreements that elections were to be held in Vietnam in five years and it was also stated that no country was to set up military bases in Vietnam. America did not agree with this but said that she would not disturb it by force—she went on to violate both these agreements. America said that she sent aid to the government in Vietnam but as the government was run by an American puppet the Americans were just giving themselves help in the job of taking over Vietnam. Gradually more and more American troops went to Vietnam all of them being called advisors even when the country was involved in a definite war.
>
> The Vietcong were trying to liberate the country from the french and afterwards the Americans. Not all of them were communists some of them just wanted what should have been their right to be

able to rule their own country. But the Americans mad on the thought that communists should be hunted out and destroyed went into the job of routing out the Vietcong only to be defeated nearly twenty years later.

Vietnam became a testing place for all the new weapons of the day. The Americans in the South and the Vietcong to some extent, the North being supplied by the Russians and the Chinese. At one stage it was thought by some people that a nuclear bombardment of Vietnam was likely and that it would have started a third world war. Throughout the sixties and into the seventies the war raged in Vietnam. The Americans were now in a position extremely difficult to get out of.

Like Susan's piece about adoption, this is competent transactional writing. Steve has the situation in a sufficiently clear perspective as far as the sequence of events goes to be able to make a consistent interpretation about what happened. We may not necessarily agree with it, but in terms of the development of his writing ability, it is well on the way to being for a public audience rather than more narrowly for the teacher.

The most difficult piece of writing that he had tackled by the middle of the fourth year was a highly speculative piece called 'The Ultra Terrestrials'. In the commentary which he did for us on this piece he writes:

> This for people who do not understand the title is about U.F.O.s and is one of the few pieces of work in which I put forward ideas that are my own and not compare ideas of other people ... Incidentally having gone into this piece of work with an open mind then disbelieving that they exist I come out of it with an open mind. But this is a subject into which I do not want to go too deeply. I have already stopped reading one book because of the complete change I found it was having on all my ideas. By change I mean a complete re-structuring from what we know at present. It may have been written by a raving lunatic on the other hand it may not. But whether I know U.F.O.s exist or not there is nothing I can do.

Restructuring our view of the universe (and our own place in it) can be a painful process whatever our age. We can sympathise with Steve's rather baffled resolution to stick to subjects which are not so unsettling—but the struggles in the writing that he did, in an effort to come to terms with a disturbing new theory, interest us for two reasons. First, the speculations, derived from the idea of an 'electro-magnetic spectrum', are interesting in themselves—and fraught, as Steve can see, with new possibilities about the perception and the interpretation of reality. Second, they are also being handled in written language by a fourteen year old who has developed sufficient confidence in his own capacity to reason things out, to be willing to take on this kind of thinking about an abstract concept. Remember how in the original Writing Research samples, speculative writing only appeared in the seventh year and was rare even then. Steve, at fourteen, is able to speculate like this:

> —We can say that we have four dimensions to move around in, we can move forward, sideways, upwards (if it was not for gravity) and we can and are doing all the time, move in time.
>
> If we take this as our definition for these dimensions that say for two ordinary people to live without their lives overlapping while one of these dimensions is the same, then at least some of the others must be different.
>
> —But what as we asked earlier are the dimensions of movement of these U.F.O.s? We could take a graph like this to give them two dimensions:

```
        │ C
 energy │ B
        │ A
        │
────────┼────────────────────────────────
        │ cosmic   visible   vector   etc
        │ rays     light     waves
        │
        │ ──▶ electro magnetic spectrum
```

> but this would not in fact work because as we understand it if we get the two life forms A and B then if they are separated only by their energy they would add to become life C. We could have beings of different frequencies having different energy but no two beings of different energy but the same frequency. We must also remember that the amount of energy these beings have is proportional to their frequency at the time and the higher that frequency is, the more energy they have. On the face of it it would seem that this is not one

of the other dimensions. But we must remember that on earth with humans there could be a point where all four dimensions became the same without the two human beings becoming merged into the same thing but with more energy. Still, we have two possible dimensions surely there must be more?

—What we could possibly have existing is an indefinite number of plains of life at different points on the electro magnetic spectrum there is no reason why they should deliberately come into the part of the spectrum of another life form but this might not be an intentional action just as we might do the same unintentionally to other life forms.

There is nc reason why these life forms should not be parallel to ours but just on a different plain of existence. They could have the same problems—have as much of the electro magnetic spectrum as us but just be in a different part of it. They might know as much as we do about U.F.O.s and could possibly see our aircraft which would to them appear as U.F.O.s.

—All the time we have been talking about life from a different frequency what do we mean by life? Life as we know it, well what is this—it is something that acts rationally we might think yet when we think about it there is nothing that acts more irrationally than a human being. Perhpas we could define life as something that is not at all logical rather than a machine that is logical. But this question is really too complicated to answer in a few words and it might be better to leave this question to poets and philosophers.

Steve ends up out of his depth—in fact he's never really been sure of his ground from the start (which after all is one of the features of speculation). But the value of the writing surely is that it provides him with a medium through which he can handle and try to make sense of these ideas which both interest and disturb him. Writing them down helps to hold them still enough (almost) for him to try and make them fit with what he knows about physics. What stimulated him to work at the possibilities in writing seems to be the sense that he was breaking new ground—trying to form his own theories from what he had read: 'one of the few pieces of work in which I put forward ideas that are my own . . .' Expressing one's own *opinions* is a relatively easy job, formulating one's own *ideas* is a different thing altogether; perhaps many teachers who read this pamphlet will have come across pupils in their fourth and fifth year in school who have been able to launch out into this kind of speculation but so far we have seen very few examples of such writing in this age range; for us Steve's struggles represent a considerable and encouraging achievement.

Are pupils likely to write more—and more discriminatingly—if the range of writing audience and writing function is held open rather than closed down as they move up the secondary school? It is difficult to answer this question at all categorically, especially as the general pattern seems to be towards narrowing the range in the face of external examinations. Nevertheless the question remains: is a preponderance of classificatory transactional writing produced for a teacher who is regarded predominantly in an examiner/assessor role either educationally necessary or desirable? For the students whose written work we have used in this pamphlet, the reverse appears to be the case. They have demonstrated that when it is appropriate they can take up such informational writing adequately, but in addition they have also taken up other options—to write expressively, thoughtfully, sometimes tentatively about topics which genuinely concerned them. They have shown that it is possible to write for an unknown public audience. They have also, by their own account, engaged in using written language in the process of self-discovery, putting down their thoughts into words that can be read and returned to, as a valuable aid to learning.

from Writing in Science

At the beginning of May 1974 the Project Team held a seminar for science teachers at Wansfell College in Essex. We invited teachers whom we had already met through our work in schools to join us for a weekend to consider the use of writing in science teaching and learning. In the event seven science teachers were able to come, and also the Head of King Harold School at Waltham Abbey. We were fortunate in having with us biology, chemistry and physics specialists, all of whom were also involved in running combined science courses for the 11-13 age groups—and in some cases up to 'O' level.

We had asked those participating to bring samples of writing in science from their schools and these, together with some of the data and findings from the previous research project, *The Development of Writing Abilities, 11-18*, gave us common reference points for our discussion.

Because, for two and a half years, we have been chiefly concerned with the 11-13 age group, the majority of the writing samples quoted here lie within this range. Nevertheless, several of the papers in this pamphlet do in fact cast forward in their arguments.

This was the first intensive workshop with interested teachers from a single school subject that our Project had organised. The discussion of the implications of the Writing Research findings, together with consistent reference to actual work in schools, generated a sense of opportunities opening out. We hope that some of these possibilities will be communicated in the papers in the pamphlet, but we know that the most significant insights occurred—as might be expected—in the talk: when (necessarily) transformed into explicit transactional writing, the excitement, or concern, demonstrated in the spoken utterances has largely disappeared. We have decided therefore to begin with some contributions to the discussions that took place in the first two sessions. They are presented disconnectedly.

ITEMS FROM THE OPENING DISCUSSION

— Two considerations that face science teachers:
  1) the child's own language and where he is;
  2) the body of scientific knowledge that you want the child to learn.
— What do kids see experiments as being for? 'Is it a real problem for me to solve?' or 'What does the teacher want me to do?'
— Genuine science outside school is about solving real problems.
— There are difficulties sometimes about using real situations first—when the apparatus found in a real situation is often so complicated—where artificial situations can be so much simpler . . .
— There are dangers of the teacher-as-expert inevitably putting the child in a situation which only makes sense when you know beforehand what you're trying to do. We don't provide children with the situation where *their* processes, not ours, structure what they do.
— Worksheets look easy to the teacher, but for the kids there is a lot of thinking to be done—and discussion.
— We tend to use writing unthinkingly—i.e. in a very structured

way: 'What to do', then 'What to write'. We break writing tasks down into a number of questions to which fairly short replies are required. There is very little opportunity for open-ended writing.
I try to arrange every piece of worksheet work so that it begins with a few general questions introducing the idea and ends up with writing which brings in the children themselves. This will depend on the actual subject matter of course.
We felt strongly that a mixed ability situation would demand that the teachers' worksheets must be understandable to all the children with the main view in mind, 'Will he be able to get the answer we want him to get?', because if not it's going to be awkward for going on to the next piece of work.

Science:
Writing and Understanding—
Writing and Learning

Sue Watts

Much of the material we deal with in science is ideas; we hope that the children will develop their own ideas about the world around them. These ideas can be backed up by the evidence of their own experimental investigations and by reference to previously learned skills and facts.

Expressive language is important if we take this view of science teaching because it is closely related to thought and ideas. When a group of children is presented with a problem, many ideas, explanations, answers, suggestions for experimental work etc. arise. While experimental work is in progress children (and teacher) may talk about what is happening or what they are doing, many ideas may be thrown in, some only to be discarded almost immediately. On the whole I find children unwilling to put these ideas on paper, they do not wish a permanent record to exist. They may write a few notes for their own personal use. When they are a little more satisfied with their own ideas they may try writing as a way of sorting these out. This is illustrated by the example of writing from a group of first-formers who had been doing work on what happens to copper when it is heated (pp.19/20).

Writing done while an experiment is in progress or while observations are being made tends to be very personal; it's often a list, or set of information the child may use later. 'Writing-up' after experiments is often still very expressive, children are not always certain of their ideas. The work on the candle done by a group of first year girls illustrates the different ways in which the children decided to write about what they had done. Vicki wrote her list as she worked and left the lab. telling the others how much she had found out. Anna spent time later writing about what she had done and seen. She seems to have felt the need for a word ('technical term') to describe how the wax gets up to the flame—'... sort of climbs up ...' Michelle also uses her own ideas and, although some of her writing is not as clear as the other two examples, she has reached a stage further, she is able to generalise from her observations.

VICKI

Watching a candle burn: things I have noticed about a candle
1. It gives light.
2. If the flame is kept still it will stand up straight.
3. It gives a flame like the bunsen burner with the air hole closed but the flame on the candle is more still.
4. It has four different colours in the flame. Blue at the bottom on the wick, dark orange above the blue, yellow in the middle with a faint orange line going through the yellow, then at the top it goes orange.
5. The wax gets to the flame because the wick soaks up the wax, so if you light it, you will get a flame.
6. At the top there is a wax liquid.
7. Some of the wax has turned into a gas.
8. When you blow out a candle it gives out smoke and a burning smell.
9. When it burns wax pours down the side and goes hard.
10. As the wick burns it turns into a black cord.
11. At the end of the wick it is orange.
12. As you flick your finger through the flame, it doesn't hurt but you can feel warmth.
13. If you put a lighted spill just over the wick on the flames, it should light. This is because some of the wax turns into a gas and it escapes so if you lit it it would come alight.
14. When I put a glass vase over the flame it went out, but if I brought it up in time the flame would have stayed alight. It goes out because no oxygen could get to the flame.

ANNA

The Candle
As I look at the candle I see that the very bottom of the flame is blue then as you look higher up you can see a brownish yellow then higher

up it is a bright yellow, then when you look at the very tip of the flame it is a brownish yellow again.

If you hold your hand quite a way up from the flame, you can still feel the heat quite strongly, strong enough to make your hand sting. If there is someone walking by the candle will flicker, also if you are breathing quite close to it.

Even though the flame does not touch the wax the wax burns away. I think it is that the wax sort of climbs up the wick so it will burn the wax.

When the wax burns it does not only turn into a liquid but also into a gas. We lit a spill, then blew the candle out and put the lighted spill quite a way over the wick, then the candle lit.

We also put a tall jar over the candle and saw the flame go out as the candle had burnt up all the oxygen what a candle needs to burn.

MICHELLE

A Candle when it burns

My candle is on a slant with a black wick and white wax. The bottom and the top of the flame is orangy gold the middle is a yellowy gold. As the wick burns the wax turns to a kind of oil liquid. The liquid runs down the candle and drys to more wax.

When you blow it it flickers and that's the only time you can see smoke go up.

Outside the flame there is a kind of blue which outlines the flame from the middle of the flame to the bottom.

The wax reaches the wick by soaking up to it as paper soaks into water.

The wax when it turns to liquid it also turns to gas because when we blow the candle out all we have to do is light the liquid and a flame appears on the wick.

A candle needs air to keep it alight so if you blot out the air around it it will go out as soon as you do blot out the air, at least my one did.

I think these examples show part of a spectrum of the ways in which children write, from the straightforward list of observations to the start of generalisation and speculation. All these types of writing are important; the child begins with the observations, thinks about them and then, we hope, begins to generalise.

I feel (though as yet I have no evidence) that these are steps towards good transactional writing. I would hope that from these beginnings we would later see the child being able to sort out which is the strictly scientific content of the work and which the personal details.

We need to provide a wide range of opportunities so that there will arise different types of writing, giving pupils as much chance as possible to write. Rosemary Sherrington's stories about William Harvey (quoted on pp.24/5 below) illustrate how a different type of writing has been used; the children have still used some scientific concepts.

One of the most important aspects of science, which is often neglected in school science, is the creative. If we are hoping to encourage children to think about their science we must give them as many opportunities as possible of different ways of thinking and looking at their ideas. How many important scientific discoveries began with a 'lucky accident'? The 'lucky accident' alone is not sufficient, the scientist involved had to think up new ideas to go with the chance observation.

I feel that there is a great danger in the constant use of worksheets in science teaching. These, surely, take most of the ideas and creativity out of the child's approach to science. The automatic response of the child in school faced with a well-structured set of questions on a worksheet is to work through these, attempting simply to get the 'right answer' to each part and not thinking about anything more than is asked of him in a particular question. This will be especially so with the type of worksheet where spaces are left and answers of one or two words or a phrase are required.

Even without using a worksheet we can impose a structure of our own on the pupils. This could exclude their own ideas if we're not careful. The pupils in one of my first-form groups were heating substances to see what happened to them. I suggested that they wrote their observations in the form of a table and didn't ask them to write anything else (they know that I would read anything else if they did write more). Anna wrote her results as I suggested, it's simply a record of her observations. In addition to this she had done a piece of much more expressive writing in which she told me exactly what she liked and thought important.

I would hope that the use of expressive writing will help the children to understand and develop ideas in their science lessons. Once they understand what they're doing they will realise which parts of what they have done are 'scientifically relevant'. When the children understand this they will be able to write at higher levels of transactional writing. I would also hope that by more personal involvement in their science they will find it more interesting and exciting and thus, eventually, easier to learn.

ANNA

Last weeks	This weeks	Things that stay the same	Things that go entirely different
Copper	Zinc oxide	*Red lead* changes when heated but when cool turns back to before it was heated.	*Copper* because goes black
Copper carbonate	Ammonium dichromate		*Copper carbonate* changes to a black powder
Magnesium	Red lead	*Zinc oxide* changes colour when heated but when cool turns back to before it was heated	
Ammonium chloride	Iodine		*Magnesium* flares up and then drops off
	Lead metal		*Ammonium chloride* makes a white vapour
Cobalt chloride			*Cobalt chloride* changes colour
Copper sulphate		*Lead metal* changes into a liquid when heated but when cool turnes back to a solid	*Copper sulphate* turns white and stays white
			Ammonium dichromate turns to a greeny black and bubbles and sparks
			Iodine turns mauve and is a vapour. Vapour then disappears and glitter is left in the tube.

SOME FURTHER WORK FROM ANNA
Heating Substances

a) Today we did an experiment where we heated substances. We had a lot of funny results like the Magnesium. When we put that in the flame of the bunsen burner it flared up bright for about six seconds and then dies down. It was a metal when we put it into the flame but after it flares up it is just bits of white on the asbestos sheet. There were two other funny ones, they were Ammonium chloride (which I got in my cut) and copper. The copper one was a bit of copper in a test tube that had to be heated. (Amanda left the tube in the flame to long so the tube began to melt). The copper went black. When it was nearly cool the black stuff began to peel itself off. Underneath there was just a bright orange/red colour. The Ammonium chloride was a white powder in a test tube. When it was heated it made a white vapour up the top of tube. When it was cool the white marks were still on the test tube. We did some other experiments like, Copper carbonate, Cobalt chloride and copper sulphate. These results were not as good so I won't tell you about them.

b) Today we did some experiments following on with last weeks. There were some good ones this week one was Iodine. There was only a tiny bit of it in the test tube. When it was heated it made a deep mauve vapour up the tube with a glitter on the sides of the test tube. When it was cool the deep mauve vapour disappears and only the glitter was left. Another good one was Ammonium Dichromate. It started of as orange granules. But when heated it sparked, bubbled and began to blow out of the tube. The powder began to turn a greeny black powder. When it was cool it stayed a greeny black powder. I think the best one today was lead metal. It was a bit stronger than foil but was a deep grey and very bendy. It was not heated in a test tube but a broken evaporating dish. Miss Watts put the lead metal on to the dish and held the dish in a pair of metal tongs. The metal began to melt. It changed from colour to colour. Some of the colours were purple, red, orange, yellow, blue and green. Then Miss Watts tipped some of the liquid onto the asbestos sheet. It then turned back into a solid but different shapes. There were some other things that we done today but they they were not as good. Here is a piece of the metal. [Metal attached.]

c) Copper

Today we did an experiment finding which was the substance that was making copper turn black.

We had a small piece of copper and we had to fold it up a certain way so that the air would not get in. Then we got a hammer and hammered it down tightly to make sure no air would get in. Then we got a pair of metal tong's and held the copper over a bunsen burner. After a while it began to turn black. Then we put it down on the asbestos sheet and waited for it to cool down so we could undo it.

When it cooled down we undone it and were quite amazed as it was a copper colour.

I think that it is something in the air around the copper that gets burnt and then cling's, so that is why it goes black.

Here is the copper. [Diagram]

Worksheets—My Changing Attitudes Towards Them

Jeff Shapland

In retrospect there are two reasons why we chose to use worksheets when Countesthorpe opened in 1970:

a) to enable us to operate mixed ability groups;
b) to enable students to work at their own pace.

Our example was undoubtedly the Nuffield Foundation Resources for Learning Project. I can't remember ever doubting that this was the best way to operate. I do so now for several reasons. As regards mixed ability teaching, I taught previously in a nine-form entry *banded* comprehensive, but we taught the same content to each band in the first year. So each band did, for instance, the rock salt experiment. So why do we now think that we have to write a worksheet for it just because the pupils are mixed instead of being in bands? If we feel that our approach to the different bands was different, and that this was a necessary part of the learning process, then it is logical that we should have several different varieties of worksheets on 'rock salt' for the different kids. Apart from the fact that this introduces a form of streaming into a mixed ability situation, we should never be able to cope with the production. I can see no reason why we couldn't carry on the 'rock salt type' activity with first years in mixed ability groups without worksheets for it.

What about students working at their own speed? Two ways of operating independent learning in mixed ability groups are: (i) a topic-by-topic approach—what Reid and Booth call short term independent learning—and (ii) long term independent learning, where pupils can move as rapidly as they wish. Reid and Booth conclude[1] that long term independent learning is less likely to be successful, except in highly structured courses (perhaps physics) and that it is rarely operated. So it would seem that many of the hundreds of worksheets being produced at present are probably for use in short term (or medium term) independent learning, with all pupils say covering the topic of 'Energy', or 'Water', but with some doing it in greater depth. It would seem to me that in this situation it would not be impossible to operate without highly structured worksheets. Some written material, instructions, stimulating ideas, yes.

But there are other reasons why I became increasingly unhappy about the large-scale use of worksheets. First, because they only cater for the upper ability ranges. The average and below average are rarely stimulated by even the most attractively produced worksheet and many are less than that! Second because, although the use of worksheets frees the teacher from the central role of initiating all the activity, he is often replaced in the pupils' minds by the worksheet. I have seen kids as lost when the worksheets ran out as they used to be when the teacher didn't turn up. And, more important, the worksheets can come between the teacher and pupil, so although the teacher has more time to go to each group there is not a corresponding increase in pupil/teacher interaction. The student is often relating more to the worksheet. When I ask 'What exactly are you doing?' I often get the answer 'This bit here' (and they point to it).

Another worry is how far worksheets can encourage a scientific approach to problems, how far they can encourage a problem-solving approach. In particular, how can 'planning how to tackle a problem'[2] be encouraged if the worksheet goes on to state exactly what must be done to solve it?

And finally, but perhaps most important of all (after the science seminar at Wansfell), I am concerned at the way worksheets limit the students' use of language which could be so crucial in the learning process. If it is true that our first drafts of thinking start in the expressive and that the thrashing out of ideas in expressive language plays a crucial part in understanding, then it is clear that many of the worksheets I have written and many other people's do not (and possibly could not) make provision for this. Nuffield stated the case for pupils' records being personal back in 1966[3] but we forgot that in our enthusiasm to produce worksheets.

So what now? Can we have a bonfire of all our worksheets, sell the offset litho and banda machines and dismiss our printers? I think not. We need printed materials and for some aspects of our work we may need worksheets. I would favour the following approach. For the first three years we should hope to do without closely structured worksheets on which pupils write. Small booklets of ideas and information may be required and other resources such as heat-sealed cards. (It is interesting that this is the way things have evolved—through feeling rather than rational thought—at Countesthorpe for Years 1-3.) In addition I would hope to see the use of written language encouraged positively— especially in imaginative situations. The problem with fourth and fifth years' mixed ability work, where some are working towards 'O' level/C.S.E. and some do the subject for interest's sake only, is more difficult. In chemistry I operate long term independent learning for this age range but I am only too well aware that those who gain most are the brightest students. They forge ahead, work enthusiastically and intelligently from the printed sheets, and get a good grasp of the subject *almost without any help from me.* And that is a cause for concern! Within a group of 20-25 fourth/fifth years there will be only about four groups of four working towards exams, and probably only six groups of four overall. I would like to explore the possibility of working with the groups, setting problems to be solved, advising on experiments, discussing results, and guiding them to background reading on a teacher/student basis without the worksheets coming in between.

Independent learning without worksheets—can it be done? If it can, I think the learning situation could be very much improved;

the gulf between those who can operate with worksheets and those who can't would be narrowed, and everybody might be able to contribute to the raising and solving of the problems and we might get genuine mixed ability teaching. I intend to discuss it further with my colleagues with a view to trying it in the near future.

Notes

1. Reid D and Booth P, *Biology for the Individual* (series), Heinemann Educ. 1971
2. On the question of 'Planning how to tackle a problem' the *Nuffield Chemistry Introduction and Guide* has this to say (pp.4/5):

> *Our chief concern will be to encourage pupils to be scientific about a problem.* This means that they must have mental and manipulative skill in the exploration of a situation which, though familiar to us, is new to them. In all new situations one gropes and fumbles and is likely to make mistakes. This, however, is the exercise by which judgment develops. A pupil must have graded opportunities to be right or wrong, and he must be guided and encouraged to become better at finding out whether or not he is right. This is time-consuming at first but only time-wasting in the context of having to cover a traditional syllabus: properly organized, it brings considerable educational benefit later on. Our hardest task will be to extricate ourselves from 'the straitjacket of chronic success' and be willing to reconsider our methods. For example we have to learn to judge when to keep silent, leaving the pupil to puzzle the problem out by himself, and when to give encouragement and advice. That the pupil should see the point of experimental work is of the greatest importance. He must learn that chemicals, test-tubes, thermometers, and sources of heat and electrical energy are tools to which he should always turn to settle a point of curiosity or of speculation. He must learn that it is proper, not wrong, to have an opinion or an idea about something he observes, but he cannot begin to think he is scientific if he does not check whether his idea fits the observed experimental facts.
>
> If we are to develop science teaching along the lines of these proposals, the appropriate organization of laboratory work for classes of thirty or more will play a very important part. *Each experimental undertaking involves three EQUALLY important stages in which the pupil must take an active part*:
>   a. *Planning how to tackle the problem.*
>   b. Carrying out the experimental work.
>   c. Discussing what deductions may, and may not, be made from the results.

> ... *From the beginning they must be encouraged to think imaginatively about the problems confronting them, and to suggest further experiments and explanations.*

3. In Chapter 6 of the *Nuffield Chemistry Introduction and Guide* the authors raise two questions about writing: 'What is the purpose of keeping a record? Does the pertinence of this exercise change as the pupil gets older?' They suggest the following major considerations (pp.105-107):

> The chief reason for making a pupil put something on to paper is to sharpen his understanding. What must be avoided is turning it into a chore and only the teacher can tell whether or not the written work is of value.
>
> The building up of a notebook is in most cases enjoyable and stimulating if it is *personal*; this can rarely be so if the material is dictated and made uniform throughout the class.
>
> ... In the early part of the course, much that is done does not need permanent record. This not only applies to details of practical techniques, such as filtering and evaporating, but also to class discussions, and to many quick exploratory experiments. Young pupils want to be doing most of the time and must not be hampered by too much written work, which they often find difficult, and at which most of them are very slow. They should be encouraged to regard their notes as diaries in which they record, briefly and simply, the more important things that they do, and the significant speculations and conclusions that lead to and emerge from their experimentation. A good deal of guidance from the teacher will be essential at the beginning of the course. Methods of guidance—half-completed tables or sentences on the blackboard, skeleton notes, help in drawing labelled diagrams— are well known. However, as with all diaries, the individuality of the compiler will soon become apparent and some pupils will want to include samples of substances that they have made (sometimes at home), cuttings and illustrations from newspapers and periodicals, chromatograms, indicator colours, charts, and a host of other items. This should be encouraged but not insisted on. It is one way in which enthusiasm and interest will show themselves; these cannot be imposed but should be fostered.
>
> ... Towards the end of the course we can say that the pupil's laboratory notebook should be a sort of journal of the progress of the work. It should contain more than a mere account of what operations he carried out and what results followed: when completed it should be a valuable account of the term's activity.

(Emphases in these extracts are Jeff Shapland's own.)

from Language and Learning in the Humanities

Like our 'Writing in Science' pamphlet this collection of writings was a planned outcome from a Seminar at Wansfell College in Essex. In February 1975, a Group of 11 teachers from geography, history and English met together for a weekend to discuss aspects of humanities teaching. They formulated their own questions in group discussion, identified their areas of concern and worked on them individually or, if their interests coincided, with each other. These papers are some of the outcomes, which we hope will help other teachers.

The thread running through all these papers is a concern with how to make learning more accessible to more students more of the time.

A Language for Life—or School?
Bryan Newton

John Colclough, the head of geography at Garth High School, Morden, was unable to join the Wansfell Seminar but instead he sent some writing which he had asked his 4th and 5th year students to do on 'The Importance of Language in Education'. 'Asked' is not the usual educational euphemism—the students were free to write or not. John gave very little explanation although in the case of the 5th year students he did suggest they define 'language' and 'education' and try to marry the two together—but there is little observable effect on the writing. He was pleased with the response—he received 33 pieces of writing.

In most of the writing there is an impressive confidence—not so much in what is said as in the manner of saying it—a sense of putting forward a valid point of view based on the writer's experience and knowledge. Only one girl expressed the anxiety that she had perhaps not satisfied the expectations of the teacher—that there might be a right answer which she hadn't found:

> When we were given this piece of work, I did not understand it fully, but I was asked to write my opinion—so here it is—even if it is not quite the work that was required.
>
> (Annabelle)

The power of the school as an institution was also evident in a number of responses which suggested the inseparableness of the school and education:

> In order to incresae your vocabulary you must increase your knowledge, and you only receive this new knowledge at school, where you are educated . . . Education is where your teacher explains certain facts to you.
>
> (Paul)

This view of education reached its logical conclusion with the final statement from another student that

> It finally winds up in his examinations, whether 'O' or 'A' levels or University degrees he must be able to make it clear what he is saying or his years of education could be wasted.
>
> (Martin)

However, a more philosophical view identified a separation between school learning and other learning:

> To me education is very important. We never stop learning things all the time we have experiences, experience is learning. So, we can be educated by our senses, we remember our experiences and feelings. This broadens our outlook on life and is very important because it helps us to appreciate the quality of life. The other type of education is what basically we learn in school, that is factual events etc. These give us satisfaction in knowing them and we can be tested *exactly* to see what we know.
>
> (David)

The view of school learning as essentially concerned with facts which have to be remembered was reflected in the number of comments on the language of teachers and textbooks. If the game is transmission of information then at least it should be efficiently played. Some students thought that it wasn't:

> A teacher can go on and on about something using long complicated sentences and words, which some, but not all of the class might not understand the meaning, and at the end the class might not have fully grasped the lesson. What is the point of this. The class might say that this teacher knows his or her subject inside out, but when they are trying to pass it on to thirty students at a time, and it is not fully understood what is being taught, then it is a complete waste of time. That one person is not giving the benefit of his knowledge to all the students he or she is teaching.
>
> (Paul)

This raises not only the question of whose language—the teacher's or the pupil's?—but also the usefulness of this method of instruction as the only way of conducting lessons.

Another student made a similar point:

> Teachers when giving notes or explaining a theory, have the annoying habit of doing one of two things. They either use words which the pupils have never heard before and therefore do not know the meaning and unless they ask the teacher does not tell them but expects them to know. The other fault of the teacher is the complete opposite—they often talk and treat the pupil as though he is an infant school pupil and not a fifth form high school student.
>
> (Alan)

Teachers who habitually dictate notes are also criticized:

> In one lesson the teacher . . . just dictates to us at such a fast speed we don't have time to absorb the notes and as we don't know what we are writing it becomes very dull and boring.
>
> (Janice)

Another student put it more poetically:

> It is absolutely no good just writing reams of notes which only superficially enter one's brain. So many lessons become set in this pattern

> —the content of the notes is not remembered and the wasted paper serves only as a reminder of the wasted hours.
>
> (Karen)

However, the students did not merely criticize negatively what went on in their lessons. Arising from their comments on the teachers' language and methods they made positive suggestions for improvements. These took a variety of forms. Sometimes the contrast was made between what was seen as good and bad in the teaching they experienced, as in this comment—still on note-taking:

> I find that when a teacher dictates notes, they are much harder to understand, than a teacher who does not. As he or she, whatever the case may be, has their own way of writing the information, and sometimes it can be somewhat of a problem to understand the notes given. Whereas a teacher who does not use this method, and will only explain what is to be said I find is much more easily understood, as when it comes to write up the notes, you can write what you think and not what someone else has told you.
>
> By using this method, I find one can adapt whatever ability one has in English, to rewriting the notes, using ones knowledge. In a way that they can be understood.
>
> (Royston)

Most of the suggestions for improvement pointed to the desire of students to participate more actively in the learning process rather than just remaining as the passive recipients of teacher knowledge. The piece just quoted modestly makes this point. It was made more strongly by other students—often in connexion with their comments on spoken and written language:

> In school you do not have to use language to express your opinions a great deal. When you do have to express your opinions it is usually in written form and so you do not gain much experience of actually talking and expressing your opinions to someone else. I think we should have time in school for discussing various topics. As well as gaining knowledge by listening to others, we would also learn to inform others of our knowledge and opinions.
>
> (Deborah)

The social implications of more talking in schools were not missed either. As one student wrote:

> The use of language in education also includes the relationship between the teachers and the students.

This notion was implicit in many of the pieces of writing but one student explicitly made the link between more open discussion and a more open relationship between pupils and the teacher. Her reference to the 'natural aloofness' of the teacher seems to me a well-merited rebuke to the traditional transmission model of language:

> Unfortunately one still finds that open discussion is not really encouraged in schools until the pupil reaches an age when the teacher finds it difficult to suppress discussion anyway. I feel this is sad since a 'conversation' between pupil and teacher helps to break down both the natural aloofness of the teacher and the reluctance of more than half the class to say anything aloud. The sooner this reticence is overcome the better for all concerned and the earlier young people begin to reap a benefit from their ability to make a valid point when they need to.
>
> (Karen)

So far I have been concerned mainly with the students' reactions to their experience of language in school. However, many of the writings expressed a sense of enjoyment of the variety and power of language. It is worth noting that these celebrations of language did not occur where the students were discussing language uses in school but when they were writing in more general terms about what language can do:

> I think you get a great deal of enjoyment out of language because you can communicate with one another. I think life without language would be very dull and uninteresting. Language, oral or written, is a way of letting out your feelings and emotions... We are not isolated beings living separate lives—we all have something in common we can communicate. Progress continues because we can work things out together as a team. We can take an interest in life because we can discuss it with others.
>
> (Sheila)

Another student, Jill, in a very expressive piece of writing which moved easily between personal reminiscence and generalisations about language, acknowledged the importance of written language for practical purposes, 'for example, shopping lists, facts in Geography, Sociology or any academic subject', but she went on to say:

> I find written language most useful when writing creatively. I write quite a lot of poetry. This I do purely for myself. It brings back certain moods and feelings, memories of which I am very fond. Being able to write enables me to do this.

Turning to reading, she makes a similar distinction between school language and language to enjoy:

> I love reading books, any kind of book as long as it's in story form and not discussional or scientific or educational.

Jill concluded her writing:

> As I've said before I take language for granted but I enjoy it in all its various forms, and I suppose I wouldn't be able to live without it. It would cut out a large proportion of my own personal enjoyment. I enjoy language on its own whether created by me, or read, or just as a means of communication.

What strikingly emerges from these writings is the awareness expressed by many students of the limited opportunities for a range of language use in school—the dominance of the written language of the pupils and the spoken language of the teacher is recognized and criticized. So is the lack of opportunity for the pupils to express their own views and opinions—even in written form.

Many of these students have no doubt about the value to them of talk for 'working things out', for the enjoyment of 'communicating with each other' and for 'letting out your feelings and emotions'. And the same goes for writing, as we have seen.

In terms of written language these students' writings exemplify what they would like to promote—the opportunity to give their own views and have them taken seriously. More than that, though, it enables them to find out for themselves in the process of doing the writing what they do think. Although this process of discovery could be guessed at in many of the pieces of writing, twice it seemed to surface in the language itself:

> When discussing this subject it brings to mind...

and

> Language is technically split up into two sections; verbal language and written language. Both I simply take for granted. But by having looked over the development of those two sections, in me, language has become more important.

Learning through talking and learning through writing are pointed to in the Bullock Report as central operations in language. But the much more active part which pupils will then play in their own educative process must be recognized by teachers. Unless teachers are willing to be communicated with more often as people interested in and concerned by what other people (who happen to be their students) have to say—rather than as examiners or assessors of what has been said—and unless they are willing to allow for genuine discussion and dialogue—rather than just teacher question and pupil answer—then the Bullock Committee has recommended in vain. As one student despairingly concluded:

> Language is highly important but it is not really presented well enough in school.

'A Language for Life', as the Bullock Report was titled, was seen by these students as very different from a language for school. The task is to bring life into school. Perhaps the Bullock Committee should have asked the students how to do this.

This article first appeared in the *Times Educational Supplement* 13.6.75.

Cooperative Learning

Peter Medway and Ivor Goodson

Imagine this situation—a teacher with a group in his classroom. He spends two mornings and two afternoons with them each week. He has set up a room that reflects many of his interests and his predictions of what might interest his students. There are photographs and paintings on the wall, a record-player and records, a tape-recorder, paints and brushes, as well as books and resource kits. It's a deliberately designed environment for learning.

It's noticeable that the teacher relates differently to different groups and individuals. Some he leaves alone, with others he sits down and looks at what they've done and makes vague situation-maintaining remarks. "Yes, that's good, go on". With others he's engaged in specific and animated point-by-point argument, explanation, planning, disagreement. With one group he appears serious, with others the relationship seems to be conducted through jokes, insults and repartee.

What is going on is cooperative learning—cooperation between teacher and student. There is also cooperation among the students, but we want to single out the relationship between the teacher and either individual students or small groups of friends. It's cooperative in that teacher and student look at a topic together, each presenting their own view to the other, feeling their way through dialogue towards a common perception.

Cooperation is not a euphemism, a gentler way of doing the same old thing, only by persuasion rather than imposition. The implied equality is meant to be taken seriously. The learning relationship, starting on the teacher's side with a commitment to reciprocity, progresses (when all goes well) to the point where it is experienced as a reality.

A cooperative learning experience that reaches the crucial

learning threshold might pass through three stages. After "browsing" in the "environment" the student eventually says "I want to do something on the Second World War." He gets the reply "O.K. Get started. Here's some books and magazines, there's a filmstrip you can look at." Then follows a period during which the teacher can feel quite anxious about what's going on. There may be a lot of copying out of books, drawing pictures, unrelated bits and pieces of knowledge being collected — useless knowledge it may seem, and so it may be. But what may be going on is a process of exploration in which the student, often unconsciously, feels around the topic to locate the real source of its attraction for him — some difficulty or worry or preoccupation or powerful feeling relating to it.

The teacher watches all this and tries to detect underlying themes and concerns in the student's busy activity. At the same time he tries to gently maintain it and restrain himself from criticism. By now the student is beginning to get clearer about what it is in the topic that really interests him and tries to bring it into focus. "So what you're really on about is the casual pointless way people could get killed, in ways that couldn't make any sense to them. You live your whole life, have an education, a family, fillings in your teeth, and end up in a ditch after some minor skirmish with an unimportant enemy outpost that was going to withdraw one minute later anyway." The teacher goes on to suggest further ways of exploring this central interest.

The student is now experiencing the satisfaction of successfully getting into the topic for himself and bringing it under control. He's developed tenacity and perseverance, makes statements he can back up, suggests hypotheses with confidence, and can improvise from knowledge.

The project is out of the intensive care unit and can be subjected to rough handling — the teacher can speak his mind without fear of killing it stone dead or putting the student down. The relationship has become robust and stimulating to both sides. The student is interested in the teacher's opinion of his work, enjoys his company and challenges him: the teacher has got interested in the student and the topic (about which he now knows a lot more than he did). Both now feel the mutuality which started off as an abstract ideal.

This is the stage of synthesis. The student has a perspective on the whole topic which may be expressed in a piece of writing that integrates generalizations, facts, attitudes and his whole view of the world. The final writing or presentation will express the dynamic vigour of the reconstruction of knowledge that has gone on.

This example shows what may happen to the inquiry mode of learning in a cooperative classroom context, but we would expect to find the same sort of stages where the learning mode consisted of, say, the writing of stories or poems. Here, too, there is often a theme or general underlying question running through a series of superficially unconnected pieces of writing. The location and definition and exploration of this theme constitute the breakthrough into learning that we are after.

Such a theme can only work itself to the surface where the student has the initiative in undertaking pieces of writing and in dictating the sequence. It can only happen where a teacher is not imposing tasks and the student is free to undertake the activity which seems right to him at the time, even though he cannot justify it. Which is not, of course, to say that the creation of these conditions guarantees that learning will then occur—only that it then has a chance to.

Many teachers looking at this set-up would be worried. The students are deciding on the context of the course. How does the teacher ensure that all the learning isn't trivial, that important things are brought to the student's attention and learnt about, that the student doesn't remain in ignorance of vast areas of human knowledge?

We would question the assumption which always seems to lie behind statements of this kind of worry—that the prevailing mode of teaching is somehow immune from such criticism, and actually achieves balance, seriousness and so on. While there are thousands of teachers who make lists of the important things their students should know, and design courses accordingly, they rarely make them stick in the classroom. The "important things" don't end up known—not to most students, not in any real sense. The scheme of knowledge (or of awareness of sensitivities) in the teacher's head simply does not reappear intact in the heads of the 30 students. He can decide what he likes, but it's all to no avail if the student doesn't go along with it.

The teacher may have a strong sense of what is important and what is trivial, but in practice he's dependent on what the student finds important—and that's a matter of deep personal response and not of intellectual assent to the teacher's "good reasons" for studying whatever it is. The teacher may make decisions about what to teach, but the student decides what is learnt—and he may at one and the same time not be learning most of what the teacher teaches, and be intensively and actively learning things of which the teacher has no inkling. The glaring fact about contemporary school life is surely the predominant failure of teachers to teach many children the things they consider everyone should know.

Students in fact take up from the teacher's material whatever meshes with their idiosyncratic concerns and interests at the moment. With the rest they either go through the motions in a perfunctory way; or "learn" conscientiously and then, because they have found no personal meaning in the learning, proceed to forget it again; or reject outright.

What needs explaining is why teachers persist in teaching their own content when the failure rate is so conspicuously high. Scheme after systematic, structured scheme is rolled to the front, no sooner to be committed to action than it is revealed yet again to be completely at the mercy of those it was supposed to bring under its control. The teacher watches dismayed or even, sometimes, carries on completely oblivious as it gets dismantled, rearranged, cannibalized, customized, transmuted and subverted by the subjective perceptions and motivations of the army of individual students. Bits are carried off for uses never intended by the manufacturer, materials from outside get welded on, whole systems of intricate machinery are tossed nonchalantly on the scrapheap. And the teachers, never giving up, go back to the drawing board—to produce Mark N of the same vehicle.

Maybe it is because experience has taught them to have low expectations of success. Children being what they are, you will never grab more than 40 per cent. Or it may be the illusion we all carry round with us that we can eliminate the failures if only we are given a little longer, if we work at it a bit harder, present the stuff a bit differently, use better material. It is a myth: we cannot and we do not. The model is wrong. Because it does not allow constructive feedback, it works against positive identification of individual failures to learn, and hence against any redefinition that such identification might suggest.

What is learnt should be what is important, and not what is trivial. This aim is not achieved by most teaching, but it stands a chance with cooperative learning. But we would want to look very critically at the idea of "important knowledge". We do not feel able to specify it in terms of topics, nor do we think any topic is intrinsically either important or trivial. Important knowledge is knowledge that is mobilized in the attempt to answer big questions: questions that are general in scope, that concern the pattern rather than the detail, that are about things that affect many men rather than a few, a lot of the world rather than a bit.

We maintain that all children are not only capable of being interested in these questions, but actually at some level want to know the answers to them. They want to know what the world is and what they are in it. Many older people have become numbed and incurious: they long ago lost confidence in their ability to make sense of more than their own corner of the world. For this, schools are partly to blame: by presenting knowledge in inappropriate forms as something fixed and established, to which you have a duty rather than which is there for you, they have prevented the possibility of its being seen as the very thing the child is looking for, the means of answering his unspoken questions.

Cooperative learning, unlike the prevailing methods, allows the student to "come to terms" with the school. He can come to to understand by experience and through dialogue how teachers deal with "knowledge". The teacher's knowledge is not something massive and fixed; it can be challenged and reinterpreted in ways that reveal new meaning for both student and teacher. The cooperation is a spiral process. The student kicks the ideas around, comes back to the teacher with a new set of questions, the teacher applies his knowledge to the student's problem, thus restructuring it for himself, the student takes it away again, and so on.

In secondary schools the student is seldom given the opportunity to come to terms in this way. Every time the bell rings, a new prepackaged and predigested segment appears. The assumption is that somehow the student understands the rationale for the learning pattern, or does not need to understand it; he already knows, or he can manage without knowing until PhD stage, why history, biology and French hold the key to his understanding of the world.

In the traditional school the tension between the knowledge, values and perceptions of teacher and taught often occasions deep conflict, or at least mutual incomprehension. In cooperative learning this tension, the disparity of views, is acknowledged, becomes an object of attention for both parties, and in fact provides much of the dynamic for the learning process—which in turn is now seen in its true light, as much more a matter of changing the way one represents the world to oneself than of simply receiving new information. Consequently the teacher has to learn to accord the student's knowledge and perceptions the same status and validity as his own, and to realize that, against all that his upbringing and training have told him, "academic learning", far from being synonymous with education, may often be the least hopeful starting-point for establishing an educational situation in the classroom.

This article first appeared in the *Times Educational Supplement* for 20.6.75.

Some Relevant Books

*Barnes, D., Britton, J. and Rosen, H., *Language, the Learner and the School*, Revised edition, Penguin, 1971

*Britton, J., *Language and Learning*, Penguin, 1972

**Britton, J. N. et al., *The Development of Writing Abilities, 11-18*, Macmillan, 1975

*Burgess, C. et al., *Understanding Children Writing*, Penguin, 1973

Jones, A. and Mulford, J. (Eds.), *Children Using Language*, O.U.P., 1971

*Martin, N. et al., *Understanding Children Talking*, Penguin, 1976

*Martin, N., D'Arcy, P., Newton, B., Parker, R., *Writing and Learning Across the Curriculum 11-16*, Ward Lock Educational, 1976

Rosen, H., *Language and Class*, Falling Wall Press, 1972

Rosen, C. and H., *The Language of Primary School Children*, Penguin, 1973

*Available from Boynton/Cook
**Available from NCTE